THE
GOVERNORS
OF
ALABAMA

THE PELICAN GOVERNORS SERIES

The Governors of Louisiana, by Miriam Reeves
The Governors of Alabama, by John Craig Stewart
In Preparation
The Governors of Texas, by Ross Phares

THE
GOVERNORS
OF
ALABAMA

By

John Craig Stewart

PELICAN PUBLISHING COMPANY
GRETNA 1975

**Library of Congress Cataloging in
Publication Data**
STEWART, JOHN CRAIG.
    The Governors of Alabama.
    Bibliography: p. 227
    Includes index.
SUMMARY: A biography and history of the
    Governors of Alabama from earliest times
    to present.
1.   Alabama—Governors—Biography. *1.*
    Alabama—Governors—Biography.   I. Title.
F325.S8   976.1'00992   (920)   75-8763
ISBN: 0-88289-067-0

Manufactured in the United States of America

Published by Pelican Publishing Company, Inc.
630 Burmaster Street, Gretna, Louisiana 70053

Designed by Oscar Richard

Contents

Acknowledgments

Acknowledgments, along with heartfelt thanks, are herewith expressed to the following:

My wife, Lila, whose patient and tireless efforts made the whole task infinitely easier. She not only totally researched the complex colonial period, but she also wrote the first draft of that section. She edited and typed the final draft *en toto*. It is truly her book as well as mine.

My cousin Albert Craig, Jr., librarian for Alabama's Department of Archives and History, who so generously and painstakingly furnished me with necessary facts and details which I would have been hard put to find elsewhere.

Sally (Mrs. Kenneth) Kuzenski, whose charm and good will brought me to my publisher.

Finally, a special compliment is due the late A. B. Moore, dean of the Graduate School and history professor for many years at the University of Alabama. His 1934 text, *History of Alabama*, revised edition, was an absolutely indispensable source. In fact, it is the only extant comprehensive and well documented history of the state above the secondary school level, or the only one that I was able to discover.

The quotations in this volume from Moore's *History of Alabama* are included with permission of the publisher, the University of Alabama Press, and the copyright holder, Mrs. A. B. Moore.

The quotations in this volume from Charles Summersell's *Alabama History for Schools* are included with permission of the publisher, Viewpoint Publications, Montgomery, Alabama.

All photographs are reprinted with permission of the Alabama State Department of Archives and History, except the following: Cadillac, courtesy Mrs. Tom Rand and the Dixie Press, Gulfport, Mississippi; George Johnstone, courtesy the National Maritime Museum, Greenwich, England; George C. Wallace, courtesy the Governor's Office, Montgomery, Alabama; and de Galvez, Miro, and Carondelet, courtesy Pelican Publishing Company.

THE
GOVERNORS
OF
ALABAMA

1

The Indians
(Time Unrecorded)

Alabama first belonged to the Indians. They held to distinct domains and guarded their borders as jealously from others not of their nation as did the French from the British or the Spanish from the Americans in later years.

In the time immediately preceding the white man's dominance of the land, there were at least four Indian nations within what is now Alabama—Creeks (Muscogees), Choctaws, Chickasaws, and Cherokees. Within these nations were various tribes and families bound by loyalties and provincial allegiances for generation after generation. They were not nomads.

One chieftain can assuredly be classified as a ruler in the best sense of governorship. He is Tuskaloosa (Black Warrior), giant leader of the Maubilan tribe, which fought to the last man against the marauding soldiers of De Soto in the tragic battle of Maubila in 1540.

Certainly, there were many Indian "governors" in terms of power, position, and prestige. But they did not practice the art of writing letters or journals or diaries, and their moments in history are lost to us.

This is simply a recognition that in the time before the Europeans came, the Indians ruled the land that is Alabama; they were the first governors.

2

The French
(1701–1763)

Although the Spanish made earlier explorations and temporary settlement in what is now Alabama, the French were the first to set up a lasting colonial system.

The Treaty of Ryswick in 1697 ended the War of the Grand Alliance, with the implicit allotment of the Atlantic seaboard to England and of interior America, from Canada to the Gulf, to France. France then revitalized de La Salle's dream of colonizing the land he had named Louisiana along the mouth of the great Mississippi.

Pierre le Moyne, Sieur d'Iberville, was commissioned by the French marine minister, Pontchartrain, to set up the first colony. Iberville sailed from France October 24, 1698, with four supply-laden ships and 200 men. In January, 1699, the ships entered Mobile Bay. For the next sixty-four years, France held claim to the land.

But the French colony was not begun in 1699. Instead, the ships proceeded westward until they reached the Mississippi River, which Iberville explored for a time. Finding no suitable spot for his colony, he retraced his route to the site of present day Biloxi, where Fort Maurepas, a temporary settlement, was constructed. In 1701, the first French capital, Ft. Louis de la Louisiane, was built at Twenty-seven Mile Bluff on the Mobile River.

IBERVILLE

Pierre le Moyne, Sieur d'Iberville, was born in Montreal, Canada, on July 16, 1661, the third son of Charles and Catherine Primot le Moyne. His father was a Canadian pioneer, whose sons were initiated early into positions of leadership in the raw, often violent life of New France. At age fourteen, Iberville became a midshipman in the French navy, the beginning of a distinguished naval career, highlighted by his campaigns against the English in the Hudson area and by his assignment to found the French colony of Louisiana.

Iberville brought his younger brother Jean Baptiste, Sieur de Bienville, with him on the first crossing. His brother Chateaugue and cousin Pierre Dugue, Sieur de Boisbriant, came on the second; brother Serigny, cousin Sainte Helene, and inlaw St. Denis followed. All contributed to the history of the colony. Le Moyne nepotism was a distinct advantage for young Louisiana.

Iberville was never a "governor" of the colony. He was more. He was ambassador between the swamp frontier and the splendid court of Louis XIV; he captained the vessels bringing supplies of survival across the Atlantic; he was advocate, founder, and leader of that first colonial effort.

Iberville was married in 1693 to Therese Pollet and subsequently became the father of four children. He died of yellow fever July 9, 1706, while his ship was in port at Havana, Cuba.

BIENVILLE
(1701–1713; 1718–1724; 1733–1743)

Jean Baptiste le Moyne, Sieur de Bienville, was the founder of Mobile, the first permanent colonial settlement on Alabama soil, and the governor of the land for a total of twenty-two years.

Bienville was born in Canada on February 23, 1680, the eighth son of Charles and Catherine Primot le Moyne. His parents died when Bienville was young, and he lived in the home of his brother Charles, Baron de Longueil. He became Sieur de Bienville on the death of his brother François, who was killed in a conflict with the Iroquois.

Bienville's idol was his brother Iberville, nineteen years his senior. Bienville entered service on Iberville's ship at age twelve, thus beginning a respectable naval service and a liaison between the brothers which culminated in the great adventure and challenge of planting a French colony on the Gulf Coast.

Following the Peace of Ryswick and the end of fighting between the French and British in Canada (Bienville was seriously wounded in the Hudson conflict), Iberville was given his directive by Pontchartrain to explore the Mississippi and set up a colony. Eighteen-year-old Bienville came with him.

Bienville was active in the exploration from the beginning. He apparently had a penchant for learning the Indian language, an invaluable aid in setting up trade agreements with them. Mobile became the seat of Indian congresses at which the Indians, particularly the Choctaws, were feted and honored with gifts and the calumet was smoked. Even after the capital was moved to New Orleans, the Indian congresses continued at Mobile.

When Iberville departed the fledgling settlement at Ft. Maurepas to return to France, he left Sieur Sauvole de la Villantry in command and appointed young Bienville his second. On his return, Iberville brought royal commissions for both. Following Sauvole's death from fever in 1701, Bienville became governor.

One of the first decisions facing Bienville was selection of a site for a permanent capital of Louisiana. He chose Twenty-seven Mile Bluff on the Mobile River, and in 1701 construction began on a fort and a few rough hewn buildings. The settlement, inhabited by about 150 persons, was named Ft. Louis de la Louisiane, for the glory of Louis XIV. Simultaneously, fortifications and a supply depot were built on Dauphin Island (Port Dauphin, in honor of the dauphine), which at that time had an excellent deepwater harbor and was strategically located to guard Mobile Bay from the Spanish marauders in Florida and the British buccaneers in the Gulf.

Bienville tried to convince his colonists to adopt the Indian crops and methods of farming in order to make the colony more self-sustaining. But there was a shortage of horses, and the colonists—and most of the intervening governors—were more interested in fur trading and quick returns, trusting in the quixotic arrival of supply ships, than in the slow, painstaking project of farming.

In 1706, Iberville died. Not only was the personal loss great for Bienville, but his prestige at the French court fell. In 1708, a new governor, De Muys, embarked to supplant him, but De Muys died en route and Bienville remained in office.

The problems were vast in the crude, swampland capital, including the elusive enemy, yellow fever. Floods too took their toll. In 1711, the entire settlement was inundated, and Bienville determined to relocate the capital at a more desirable site. He moved the settlement downriver to the site of present day Mobile, where the river flows into the bay. A fortification was built on the banks of Mobile River, with the town squared in around it. Royal, Dauphin, Conti, St. Francis, and St. Louis are streets named by Bienville which are yet extant.

About 400 inhabitants lived in the capital, including the military, who were the top echelon of colonial society, a few Capuchin missionaries, artisans, and women. In 1704, the ship *Pelican* had brought the welcome cargo of twenty-three marriageable girls outfitted by the king with caskets or small trunks carrying their dowries, thus giving them the name Casket Girls. The quality of life then became a little more domestic and genteel, but the populace at large still came from France's bower of adventurers, refugees, and misfits.

Bienville's first period as governor ended in 1712 when the French colony was leased by the war-impoverished Crown to a wealthy French merchant, Antoine Crozat. Bienville was demoted to lieutenant governor; Antoine de la Mothe, Sieur de Cadillac, supplanted him as governor.

Apparently, Bienville courted Cadillac's daughter, but it did not lead to marriage. Bienville never married anyone. Whatever happened, Bienville incurred the wrath of Cadillac, and he was assigned constant field duties, particularly to trouble spots with the Indians, often undermanned. In 1714, Bienville was sent to build Ft. Toulouse at the fork of the Coosa and Tallapoosa rivers as a fortification against the British, who were coming over the mountains and encroaching on the lucrative Indian fur trade.

In 1717, Cadillac departed Mobile, only to be replaced by another governor, L'Epinay. The ships bringing Governor L'Epinay to Port Dauphin also brought a royal grant of Horn Island to Bienville and the cross of the Order of St. Louis, a prestigious, flamboyant decoration. (This was the only award ever conferred on Bienville.) In 1718, Antoine Crozat returned his commercial rights to the Crown, L'Epinay returned to France, John

Law's Mississippi Company became the new landlord of the colony, and Bienville again became governor.

John Law, a refugee Scotsman and financial wizard, sold millions of shares in his Mississippi Company; in fact, he oversold. But for a few years Louisiana was a boom country and Law was the man of the hour in France.

Men and money poured into the colony, and shipload after shipload of slave labor arrived. Spain and France complicated the problems of the frontier by declaring war on each other. Taking the aggressive, Bienville and Serigny le Moyne led a major force against their Spanish neighbor in Pensacola and took the city. Chateaugue le Moyne was left in command.

Within two months, Spain retaliated with a thrust from Mexico, and Pensacola was hers again. Chateaugue was imprisoned in a Havana dungeon until the war ended. In time, after sustaining a Spanish attack on Port Dauphin, Bienville and Serigny retook Pensacola and held it until 1720, when they returned it to Spain by treaty. The Perdido River marked the boundary between the two powers—a boundary which would be a source of major dispute in later Alabama history.

As the Mississippi and its tributaries were explored and settlements established (notably that of New Orleans in 1718), Mobile decreased in importance. Actually, the death blow had come with the 1717 hurricane which had washed a giant sandbar into the harbor of Port Dauphin, eliminating its deepwater capacity. Bienville moved the capital, first to old Biloxi in late 1720, then to New Orleans in 1722.

Mobile remained the largest city in Louisiana for a few more years, and Ft. Conde continued to be a strong fortification. But, except for the Indian congresses which continued to be held there, Mobile lost its influence as a leading frontier settlement.

The Mississippi bubble finally burst, and John Law fled penniless from France, leaving a trail of bankruptcies behind him. Accusations resulting from the financial fiasco inevitably fell on Bienville. In 1724, he was relieved of his office and recalled to Paris to stand before the court.

Accompanied by his brother Chateaugue, Bienville sailed for France. The Paris court absolved Bienville from charges made against him, but it stripped him of all authority relative to Louisiana. For ten years, he resided quietly in Paris while across the Atlantic, Louisiana slipped to the edge of ruin. Finally in 1733, the Crown reinstated Bienville as governor once again; he returned to Louisiana where he was welcomed as the patriarch of the colonials.

The plague of Bienville's last decade as governor was the impaired relations with the Indians. The Natchez were virulent enemies, and the Chickasaws were in league with the British; even the old French alliance with the Choctaws had eroded. Bienville regained in large measure the confidence of the Choctaws; as their ally he built Ft. Tombecbé on the Tombigbee River in 1736 as a major fortification for assault on the Chickasaws. The battle that ensued at Ackia was a total defeat for the fifty-six-year-old Bienville. Determined to diminish the Chickasaw and English victory, he finally pacified the Chickasaws through a Mississippi campaign.

In 1743, Bienville resigned his governorship of Louisiana and returned to Paris, where he lived until his death March 7, 1768.

At age eighty-six, Bienville appeared one last time in the French court, this time to plead against the cession of Louisiana to Spain and England. But Louis XV now

Pierre le Moyne,
Sieur d'Iberville

Jean Baptiste le Moyne,
Sieur de Bienville
1701–1713
1718–1724
1733–1743

Antoine de la Mothe Cadillac
1713–1716

sat on the throne, and he was more interested in the Marquise de Pompadour than in Louisiana.

CADILLAC
(1713–1716)

Antoine de la Mothe, Sieur de Cadillac, was born in Gascony c. 1656, son of a minor nobleman, Jean de la Mothe, who owned the seigneury of Cadillac, which his son inherited. His mother was Jeanne de Maleniant. In 1687, Cadillac married Marie Therese Guyon in Quebec.

Cadillac's military career in Canada was a distinguished one. He was the founder of Detroit, which he hoped to make the Paris of New France, with himself and his family at its influential center.

When he was appointed governor of Louisiana in 1711, Cadillac was disgruntled. Detroit was his province, and he had plans to make it his lifelong home. Yet the promise of quick wealth under the auspices of Antoine Crozat, the rich French merchant who had leased the colony from the Crown, made the job acceptable.

Cadillac treated the colonists haughtily, and his administration was a debacle. He incurred the ill will of the le Moyne family in Mobile, despite a brief romance between his daughter and Bienville. Upon his arrival, Cadillac had selected the large, palatial house of Chateaugue for his family. Chateaugue was out of town at the time, so Cadillac, in effect, confiscated it.

During his three years in Mobile, Cadillac futilely (and illegally) sought to tap the lucrative Spanish trade in Mexico. He was frequently away from Mobile on treasure hunting expeditions, including a trip in 1715 to

Illinois country searching for silver. However, during Cadillac's administration some good was accomplished. Under Bienville's supervision, Ft. Toulouse was founded in interior Alabama; Toulouse became a major fortification and the center of fur trade with the Indians.

In 1716, Cadillac was recalled to France and supposedly served a short time in the Bastille. Thereafter, he made his home in his native Gascony until his death October 18, 1730, at Castle Barragin.

L'EPINAY
(1717-1718)

Cadillac's replacement, L'Epinay, arrived at Port Dauphin March 8, 1717, in merchant Crozat's boats, bearing to Bienville the cross of the Order of St. Louis and a grant to Horn Island, hardly compensation for his disappointment at being passed over for governor.

L'Epinay began construction of Ft. Conde, a splendid brick structure which remained an important fortification until the Americans tore it down. But he did little for the colony. The factions created by the enmity between the le Moynes and Cadillac remained intact.

Among other unpopular acts of his short administration was L'Epinay's prohibition of rum, an effective bargaining product advantageous in the Indian fur trade. Perhaps this prohibition was beneficial to the Indians, but the traders were irked.

In less than a year, M. Crozat relinquished his lease on the colony, and M. L'Epinay was called home to France, having contributed little to the glory of France or Louisiana.

Bienville became governor again, serving until 1824.

BOISBRIANT
(1724–1726)

Pierre Dugue, Sieur de Boisbriant, a le Moyne cousin, came to Louisiana with Iberville's second supply fleet and was deeply involved in the affairs of the colony.

Boisbriant is reported to have been a hunchback, but a man of inestimable charm. Boisbriant, along with Henri de Tonty ("Iron Hand") and St. Denis, was Bienville's major advisor and aide in Indian affairs.

After one excursion in the early days from Ft. Louis, Boisbriant brought captured Alabamos back to Mobile and, with French diplomacy, gave the captives to the Mobile Indians for slaves. In another excursion, this one involving a conflict between the friendly Choctaws and the hostile Chickasaws, Boisbriant was wounded and returned to Mobile by an honorary Choctaw procession. There he recovered, reportedly nursed by a Damoiselle Boisregnaud, who had accompanied the Casket Girls to Ft. Louis and who had fallen in love with Boisbriant. Bienville apparently put a hiatus on the romance, if indeed there was one.

When John Law's company took over the lease for the Louisiana enterprise in 1718 and Bienville was reinstated as governor, Boisbriant was appointed royal lieutenant. Later, Boisbriant was made governor of the Illinois district with the mission of opening up the Mississippi as a trade route. He built Ft. Chartes on the Mississippi, 1718–1720.

When Law fled France and Bienville was recalled to Paris to answer charges against his administration of the colony, Boisbriant was called from Illinois to become acting governor.

Conditions were bad. The populace had left by the hundreds following the collapse of Law's company, declining from 5,400 inhabitants in 1721 to 1,700 in 1724. The threat of war between Spain, France's ally, and England was imminent; therefore, conflict within the colonies was a certainty. Hostility from the Indians, especially the Natchez, increased. All this occurred at the same time the Crown was reducing its military support. Nevertheless, Boisbriant ordered the colonists to supply the forts at Mobile and the new capital of New Orleans with as much ammunition as they could commandeer. Then he, too, was called to Paris to give an accounting of affairs in Louisiana.

With Boisbriant's sailing, Louisiana was without a member of the le Moyne family for the first time since Iberville's ships anchored in Mobile Bay in 1699.

PERIER
(1726–1733)

Boisbriant's successor, Etienne Perier, witnessed the last gasp of the Companies des Indes, of which the Mississippi Company was a part, in Louisiana. Although John Law had long since deserted and the organization's failure was apparent, the Mississippi Company retained its lease of the colony until 1731, when the company relinquished its privilege of trade monopoly to the king. The colony was, at last, financially destitute.

Perier had to contend with increasing conflicts with the Indians, particularly the Natchez. In 1729, Ft. Rosalie, an important trading post on the Mississippi, was the scene of a horrible massacre. Following this, the French launched a war of extermination against the Natchez.

For the first time, a policy of brutality was fostered by French colonists—slaves were rewarded for cutting the throats of enemy Indians, and four male and two female

Natchez captives were burned to death by the French in cruel warning to the enemy. Instead of subduing the Indians, such retaliation only increased hostilities. The Chickasaws sheltered refugee Natchez, while the English urged Indian attacks against the French. England even gained favor with Bienville's old friends, the Choctaws. Luckily, however, the Choctaws did not attack their French neighbors in Mobile, by then only a shadow of a town containing about sixty families.

In 1732, Perier was appointed to the Superior Council set up by the Crown in Louisiana. In 1733 Bienville replaced him as governor.

VAUDREUIL
(1743–1753)

Pierre François de Rigaud, Marquis de Vaudreuil, third son of Philippe Rigaud, Marquis de Vaudreuil, and Louise Elizabeth de Jaybert, was born in 1704 in Canada. He became an officer in the French army, honored with the cross of the Order of St. Louis. Vaudreuil was deemed a man of aristocratic bearing, luxurious tastes, and considerable ability.

Succeeding Bienville in 1743, Vaudreuil's greatest challenge was the pacification of the Indians. He held a Choctaw congress in Mobile, hoping to strengthen their support; he was successful except for the formation of a splinter group led by "Red Shoes." Vaudreuil reinforced Ft. Conde in Mobile against possible attacks. Following Red Shoes' death, however, the Choctaws once again became united allies with the French. In 1752, Vaudreuil launched a campaign against the Chickasaws. He followed Bienville's route of 1736 up the Tombigbee to Ft. Tombecbé. Like Bienville, he lost the battle and retreated in defeat to Mobile.

In 1753, Vaudreuil was promoted to governor-general of Canada, a position once held by his father. Unlike his popular governorship in Louisiana, Vaudreuil's regime in New France was involved in political intrigue. He was recalled to France in 1760 and imprisoned in the Bastille. Vaudreuil was released the following year but never regained his prestige, living in obscurity until his death in 1778.

KERLEREC
(1753–1763)

Louis Billouart, Chevalier de Kerlerec, captain in the royal army with twenty-five years active service, followed Vaudreuil as governor. He was born June 26, 1708, son of Guillaume Billouart de Kerlerec and Louise de Lansullyen. His wife, Marie-Joseph Charlotte du Bot, accompanied him to Louisiana.

Indian raids and massacres, as well as skirmishes with the British along Louisiana's border from Canada to the Gulf, marked Kerlerec's tenure. By 1756, the colonial conflicts had culminated in full-scale war between England and France—the French and Indian War in America and the Seven Years War in Europe. When the fighting was over in 1763, France had lost all her North American possessions.

Prior to the Treaty of Paris, in which the peace terms were dictated by victorious England, France had made a secret treaty with Spain. At Fontainebleau on November 3, 1762, France had ceded to her ally all of Louisiana west of the Mississippi River. Thus at the Treaty of Paris, England received the area of Louisiana east of the Mississippi to the Perdido River boundary. England also took possession of the rest of Florida from Spain, giving her dominion over the entire eastern section of the North

American continent. Kerlerec, last French governor of Louisiana, had been replaced by foreign appointees— Spanish rule west of the Mississippi, English rule to the east.

Alabama was the scene of little fighting during the French and Indian war. Most of the interior was firmly held by the Indians, and Mobile and Port Dauphin were never attacked by the British. However, the English effectively blockaded the Gulf Coast.

Even in the midst of a great war, the petty strife of politics continued in the colony. Some of Kerlerec's actions were highly disapproved of at court and ultimately led to his imprisonment in the Bastille. He died in debt and disrepute in Brittany, September 8, 1770.

3

The British
(1763–1780)

Following the defeat of the French and the Treaty of Paris in 1763, the British moved into Alabama. The Union Jack went up, while the fleur-de-lis came down— Teutonic rule, Protestant religion, and representative government, of sorts, had come to the colony. The British allowed Frenchmen who wished to remain in Mobile to keep their property and religion, providing they swore allegiance to George III. A few did.

Alabama became a part of British West Florida, the broad stretch of land from the Mississippi River on the west to the Chattahoochee on the east. The capital city was Pensacola. The area from the Pearl River to the Perdido was named Charlotte County, in honor of English queen, and the old French fort in Mobile became Ft. Charlotte. The northern boundary in Alabama was 32°28' latitude, the demarcation running just below a line from modern Demopolis to Wetumpka. North of this line was the Illinois District, inhabited mainly by Indians and traders.

Despite Mobile's strategic position at the mouth of the interior Alabama Basin, its importance as a military outpost against the Spanish in Louisiana, and despite

19

England's passion for settling her colonies, Alabama stagnated during the seventeen-year rule of the British.

JOHNSTONE
(1764–1767)

George Johnstone, a naval officer, was sent to America by George III as first governor of British West Florida. A proud man, insistent on his rights and jealous of his powers, Johnstone found his authority as governor severely limited by military controls. Even the dispensation of supplies and assignment of civil servants were dictated by military orders, and the arbitrator of these decisions, General Thomas Gage, was stationed in New York, not Pensacola.

Johnstone shared England's interest in settlers, and he wrote glowing reports of British West Florida's land and the Choctaw lands to the north. He made generous land grants, but only a few plantations were founded at this time along the Alabama rivers.

Like many of the governors sent over from Europe, Johnstone knew little of the Indians and was not very interested in learning more. He left the Indian affairs to the Indian superintendent, John Stewart, and his lieutenant, Alexander McGillivray. Through Chevalier de Monberant of Mobile, who feted the chiefs in his home, land cessions from the Choctaws and the Creeks were accomplished. Monberant was later summarily dismissed by Johnstone.

Neither Johnstone nor the other English governors, except Durnford, were particularly interested in the affairs of Mobile, except as such matters affected them personally. The man who truly governed Mobile and the Tombigbee area was Major Robert Farmar, appointed commander by George III. Farmar, too, incurred the wrath of Johnstone, who pressed court martial proceedings against him.

Johnstone, after four years of continuous quarrels with the military, left British West Florida with a record of few accomplishments and many frustrations. Montforte Browne, his lieutenant governor, then filled the vacant office as acting governor.

BROWNE
(1767–1769)

Montforte Browne succeeded Johnstone as governor, holding that office until the appointment and arrival of a new governor from England. Browne's replacement was a man named John Eliot, who committed suicide by hanging himself in his study one month to the day after taking the governor's office in May, 1769. Thus, Browne became acting governor again, holding the office a short while longer.

Browne's problems were greater than his accomplishments, centering mainly on the military–civil conflicts over authority. He was further frustrated by the lame duck power of acting governor, and his temper was a consternation to the other officials. He was involved in various duels, until restrained through a peace order from participating in such contests.

Several things of note took place during Browne's tenure. General Gage ordered all troops, except three companies of two regiments, pulled out of West Florida and relocated in East Florida, closer to the troublesome Atlantic colonies. Governor Browne protested, but his objections were ignored, and he was forced to ship out the soldiers from Pensacola. This left Ft. Charlotte with pathetic defenses. Ft. Toulouse remained in the state of ruin in which the French had left it, and Ft. Tombecbé had been completely abandoned in 1766. Alabama was for the time practically unfortified.

Meanwhile, the few English soldiers in Mobile faced the recurrent "summer sickness" which decimated their ranks. They, more than the soldiers in Pensacola and more than the French in Mobile, seemed particularly susceptible to the seasonal plague of fever and death. In 1769, Haldimand, military commander at Mobile, ordered a Dr. Lorimer to study the sickness. After six months of survey and research, the doctor recommended temperance, hygiene, swamp drainage, and relocation of troops during the summer months. Two-thirds of the approximately fifty men at Ft. Charlotte had come down with the summer sickness during his period of study. But Dr. Lorimer's recommendations were largely ignored.

Haldimand, in 1768, also ordered provincial engineer Elias Durnford to make an extensive survey and an admiralty chart of Mobile Bay, to determine its capability and usefulness for English ships. This was an impressive project and a valuable piece of work.

In 1768, court martial proceedings against Major Farmar, who had bucked Johnstone's authority, were conducted. However, a verdict of acquittal was submitted to the king, who approved it, and Farmar remained in Mobile. Farmar then was proposed to succeed Montforte Browne, whose dueling involvements had precipitated his vacating the governor's office, but Elias Durnford succeeded him instead.

DURNFORD
(1769–1770)

Elias Durnford owned a plantation in Montrose (Red Cliffs) on the eastern shore of Mobile Bay. He was more

George Johnstone
1764–1767

Elias Durnford
1769–1770

interested in Alabama and spent more time there than any other governor of West Florida. At age twenty-four, he had come to the province with Johnstone as chief engineer and surveyor. In May, 1769, Durnford returned to England where he married Rebecca Walker. He returned with his wife to West Florida as lieutenant governor. In the meantime, the governor, John Eliot, had committed suicide, and Montforte Browne was acting governor again. In late 1769, Durnford assumed Browne's position.

The most significant contribution Durnford made to Alabama was his survey and admiralty chart of Mobile Bay while he was chief engineer in West Florida. Durnford was a lawyer as well as an engineer and also served as a chief justice at times in Pensacola. He was a man of many talents and rendered distinguished service in every office he held.

Unlike his predecessors, Durnford was a friend of the military commander at Ft. Charlotte, Haldimand, and he maintained good relations with the military. Durnford urged that a summer garrison be built at Red Cliffs, just below his plantation, for all troops not essential at Ft. Charlotte. This was accomplished on a small scale, but the military did not carry out his full recommendations, as they had not carried out Dr. Lorimer's earlier suggestions. Summer sickness continued to assault the English soldiers in Mobile.

Prior to his governorship, Durnford had drawn up plans for an overland road connecting Mobile and Pensacola, with a ferry across Perdido River. As governor, he saw this project accomplished.

Durnford held the governor's office for only a year, until Peter Chester came from England to replace him. Then he resumed his activities as farmer, lawyer, and engineer.

Alabama was apparently indifferent to the American Revolution in 1776. But when Galvez sailed into Mobile from Spanish New Orleans in 1780, the shock was felt through all West Florida. Elias Durnford was commander of Ft. Charlotte at the time. His men numbered less than 300, while Galvez had a force approaching 2,000. Galvez sent his courier to Durnford requesting the surrender of Mobile on February 5. Durnford held off the inevitable until March 14, then he turned over the town to the invading Spaniards.

Durnford, his wife, and their infant son born at Red Cliffs returned to England in compliance with the terms of exit offered by Spain. There he continued a distinguished service with the corps of engineers. Durnford died of yellow fever June 21, 1794 while on assignment at Tobago, West Indies. His son was a member of his corps.

CHESTER

(1770–1780)

Peter Chester was the last British governor of Alabama and the first to have broad civilian authority. At last, military controls were confined to the affairs of the troops. This eliminated the source of constant conflict which had plagued previous governors.

Chester was a forceful man and enjoyed popularity in Pensacola. But he was not interested in the affairs of Charlotte County. Indian congresses continued to be held in Mobile, but they were supervised by Mobilians, not the governor's office. The Choctaw complaints against English grants of their land above the Tensaw, an area not ceded to the English by treaty, were ignored.

Mobilians were dissatisfied with the limited representation allowed them in the assembly in Pensacola and with the arbitrary regulation of Indian trade by the Board of Trade. As protest, in 1772 they refused to take their seats in the Pensacola assembly. Although four out of six Pensacola assemblymen sympathized with the Mobilians, Chester instructed the group simply to eliminate the presumptious Mobile district in the next election writ. This disenfranchisement led to a complaint against Chester to the king and virtual dissolution of the assembly.

But, in spite of the revolt raging in the sister colonies on the Atlantic, there was apparently no threat of rebellion in Charlotte County or elsewhere in British West Florida. A few Whig sympathizers were around, and some Tories fled from Georgia into the Tombigbee area to settle; but the Alabama colony, remaining loyal to the Crown, was virtually untouched by the events of 1776.

In 1777, William Bartram, a noted botanist commissioned in London to make a study in British West Florida, travelled throughout the Alabama area cataloging the plant life of the colony. He was impressed with the rich spectrum of native growth and moved by the hospitality shown him along his route.

But Mobile's demise continued. Chester's indifference to the area was reflected in his decision to raze Ft. Charlotte, the old fort synonymous with the history of the city, and haul the bricks to Pensacola for construction of batteries. However, the Spaniard Galvez put an end to this plan, as well as to Chester's governorship over Alabama, when he captured the city on March 14, 1780. The Americans were the ones who finally demolished the fort.

4

The Spanish
(1780–1813)

The Spanish influence in Alabama was small, and Spanish occupancy was marked by contention and confusion.

Galvez, the aggressive governor-general of Louisiana, forced the surrender of Mobile from English commander Elias Durnford on March 14, 1780. A year later, Galvez conquered Pensacola, ending English holdings along the Gulf and reinspiring dreams of a Spanish empire in the New World.

The dreams were short-lived, however, for in the Treaty of Versailles of 1783 Spain's northern border with the United States was set at 31° latitude. The English border had been 32°28' latitude. The difference was several million acres. The U.S. and Spain argued over this boundary until final acquiescence by Spain in 1795.

By 1798, so many Americans had moved into the land between 31° latitude and 32°28' latitude that the area was incorporated into the Mississippi Territory. (The northern boundary was moved to the modern Tennessee line six years later.) The so-called Ellicott Line at 31° latitude was ignored by many settlers and viewed with contempt by others. The expanding Americans intended to stretch on to the Gulf.

In 1803, the United States concluded the Louisiana Purchase. Louisiana had been transferred to France from Spain in 1800 in the secret Treaty of San Ildefonso. Napoleon then sold the area to the United States through Jefferson's emissaries.

Again, the United States and Spain were in territorial argument, the United States contending that the purchase included all the land to the Perdido River, which had been declared Louisiana's border by Bienville, and that therefore the southern tip of Alabama was part of the land retroceded to France. Spain claimed otherwise, insisting that this section of land was still hers.

Finally, in 1813, the argument became moot, when American President James Madison ordered General Wilkinson to take Mobile by force. Madison justified the action by calling it a reprisal against Spain for opening the port of Mobile to the British in the War of 1812.

The title of the United States to West Florida was confirmed in 1819, the year of Alabama statehood. United States interests had clearly dictated the acquisition.

GALVEZ
(1780–1785)

Born in Malaga, Spain in 1746 of noble lineage on both sides of his family, son of the viceroy of Mexico, Bernardo de Galvez epitomized Spain's ambition to reestablish a dominion on the North American continent. He married a native Louisiana beauty, Felicia de St. Maxtent d'Estranan, and was popular with the settlers in Louisiana.

Appointed governor in 1777, Galvez added the strategic towns of Baton Rouge, Manchac, and Natchez along the Mississippi River to Spain's holdings within the year. In 1780, he assailed the English port of Mobile and held it under siege for a month. When the pitiable English forces surrendered, Galvez claimed Mobile for the king of Spain. He bided his time in Mobile for a year, then quickly and efficiently effected the conquest of Pensacola and the end of English rule in West Florida.

Henrique Grimarest was appointed commandant of Mobile in 1781. For the most part, the affairs of the city were in the hands of the commandant, who lived year round in the city except for summer residence on Fowl River. Government under the Spanish was lax and mainly benign. The enemy English were allowed eighteen months to change their religion and allegiance or leave. Immigrant settlers from Georgia and Carolina were welcomed. Land grants were generous. The shadow of the Inquisition in Spain did not reach the Gulf Coast.

From Louisiana, Galvez was constant in support of the insurgent American rebels in their conflict against the common enemy, the king of England. In 1785, the new Congress of the United States proclaimed public thanks to the Spanish governor for his aid during their Revolutionary War. Little did Galvez know that these same rebels and this same Congress would soon be claiming Spanish Alabama as their own.

Galvez succeeded to the viceroyalty of Mexico upon the death of his father, leaving the governorship of Louisiana and West Florida and the jurisdiction of Cuba to Miro. Galvez served as viceroy until his death, little more than a year later, November 30, 1786.

MIRO
(1785–1791)

Don Estevan Rodriquez Miro was, like his predecessor Galvez, a military man. Born in Catalonia in 1744, he began service in the Spanish army as a cadet at age sixteen; his military service culminated with promotion to major general during his governorship. Miro was aide-de-camp to Galvez in the West Florida conquest, and he served as acting governor when Galvez was called temporarily to St. Domingo in a Franco-Spanish offensive against Jamaica.

Spain's policy toward the Indians, who still outnumbered the ever increasing Americans in Alabama, was one of cooperation. Miro presided over the congress held in Mobile on June 22, 1784, to which representatives of all Alabama Indian tribes were invited and with whom trade negotiations were signed.

Miro was a literate man. Proficient in French, he also attained a limited knowledge of English, which increased his popularity and influence with the provincials, as did his marriage to a native Creole girl, Celeste Elenore Elizabeth Macarty.

Miro's major problems arose from the dispute with the United States over the designated Spanish boundary of 31° north latitude and over the influx of American settlers. Asserting Spain's claim to the land, Miro ordered Ft. St. Stephens constructed in 1790 on a bluff overlooking the Tombigbee. St. Stephens soon became a thriving, prosperous community. It fell to United States ownership when the boundary question was finally settled in 1795.

The population of Mobile doubled between 1785 and 1788, reaching almost 1,800, while that of neighboring Pensacola dwindled to less than 300. Spanish residents remained few, coming almost exclusively from the governing class, the military. Most of the new population were Anglo-American, Irish, and Scottish. The French, permanent denizens of Mobile, remained the ruling so-

Bernardo de Galvez
1780–1785

Francisco Luis Hector,
Baron de Carondelet
1791–1797

Don Estevan Rodriquez Miro
1785–1791

cial substrata. Pedro Favrot, captain in the Spanish army, was commandant at Mobile.

The generosity of land grants continued under Miro and Favrot. Among family names to become part of southern Alabama geography was that of Bosarge. The original Bosarge, Joseph "Bouzage," appealed for land in "Bayou Batree" in 1790 "in order that he may live thereon undisturbed, and conceal from the eyes of the world his poverty and misery." Miro signed the land grant, and Bosarges have been in Bayou La Batre ever since.

After Miro was succeeded in the governorship by Carondelet, he continued in military service to Spain until his death in 1795.

CARONDELET
(1791–1797)

Francisco Luis Hector, Baron de Carondelet, came to Louisiana and West Florida from the governorship of San Salvador. Born in Flanders c. 1748, descended from a long line of illustrious and noble ancestors, married into a prestigious Spanish family, and having given three decades of service to his king, Carondelet brought to the provincial governorship an impressive background.

He initiated useful but expensive public works projects—street lighting in the capital city of New Orleans, a canal from Lake Pontchartrain to the Gulf, drainage of the swamps around Mobile, reinforcement of Ft. Charlotte. But he was a man of quite ordinary mentality, deficient in English and apparently ill-trained to administer or understand the myriad problems arising from the varying lifestyles and ambitions of the frontiersmen, the native Creoles, the Indian tribes, and the aggressive American neighbors.

In Pinckney's Treaty, or the Treaty of San Lorenzo, of 1795, Spain accepted 31° latitude as the northern boundary of "New Spain," and permitted American navigational rights on the Mississippi. This limited Spain's holdings in Alabama to the thin strip of coastal land, extending from just west of Mobile to the Perdido River.

But Carondelet delayed until 1797 the surrender of Ft. St. Stephens above the 31° latitude, contending that his Catholic majesty could never have meant to turn over to the United States fortifications that might well be used against his majesty's subjects.

Even after reluctant retirement below 31° latitude, Spain was still plagued with the ubiquitous American settlers; the problem was no more effectively combatted by successive governors than by Cardondelet.

Carondelet left New Orleans to become governor general of Quito in August, 1797. He died and was buried in Quito in August, 1817.

The commandants at Mobile whose appointments spanned the six years Carondelet was governor were among the most able of Spain's captains—Vincente Folch, to 1792; Manuel de Lanzos, 1792–1795; Pedro Olivier, 1795–1798.

GAYOSO
(1797–1798)

Manuel Gayoso de Lemos spoke the language of the provincials, including English, and apparently was highly skilled in diplomacy. He negotiated trade treaties with the Indians and maintained constant communication with the Americans, at the same time strengthening fortifications against their possible attacks.

Gayoso recognized the importance of Mobile's strategic location and its traditional seat of influence with the

Indians. Pedro Olivier was commandant of Mobile when Gayoso became governor and held that position until February, 1798, when Manuel de Lanzos again became commandant.

By an act of Congress on April 7, 1798, the Mississippi Territory was created and Winthrop Sargent was appointed governor. The United States continued its attempt to get Spain to cede the rest of Alabama to them. Alexander Hamilton in 1798 proposed that the United States annex West Florida and New Orleans, for Spain was an ally of France and a threat to the United States. The American settlers agreed. But annexation did not take place then, and Lanzos in Mobile and Governor Gayoso continued their efforts at containment of the Americans and holding the southern strip of Alabama in the name of Spain. But the act creating the Mississippi Territory had sounded the death knell for Spain on Alabama's shores.

Gayoso was twice married—first to Teresa Margarita Hopman y Pereira, who died shortly after Gayoso became Governor of Louisiana and West Florida, and secondly to Margaret Watts, daughter of a Louisiana planter. Gayoso, with longer life and under more favorable conditions, might have been able to strengthen Spain's tenuous hold on Alabama. However, he died in office July 18, 1798, from a virulent fever.

CASA CALVO
(1799–1801)

Sebastian de la Puerto y O'Ferril, Marquis de Casa Calvo, was appointed governor ad interim shortly after the death of Gayoso; however, it was apparently September, 1799, before he assumed the full powers of the office.

While Casa Calvo occupied the governor's chair in Louisiana, his mother country across the Atlantic was entering into another secret agreement with France. This time it was the secret Treaty of San Ildefonso, signed in 1800, in which Spain retroceded to France the Louisiana Territory it had received in 1762 in the secret treaty signed at Fontainebleau.

These treaties illustrate how the fate of the colonies, from the earliest French settlement at Ft. Louis, were dependent on the ambitions, politics, and wars of mother countries thousands of miles across the ocean. Like pawns, the colonies were played to save the queen.

However, in the case of Louisiana, it is unlikely Spain could have kept it, even if the ministers in Madrid had not given it to Napoleon; for the Americans were her territorial enemies, and they were not across an ocean, but across a creek, and they negotiated with the musket, the ax, and the plow.

The Americans were the major problem Casa Calvo had to deal with, and the same was true for the commandants in Mobile. Manuel de Lanzos was serving his second term when Casa Calvo came in; he was succeeded by Joaquim D'Orsono in November, 1800.

Casa Calvo came to Louisiana in 1769 with General O'Reilly's army and frequented the area thereafter. In 1803, he was appointed joint commissioner with his successor, Governor Salcedo, to transfer Louisiana to Napoleon's envoy, M. Laussat. Still Casa Calvo stayed in the area, even after Napoleon sold Louisiana to America.

In January, 1806, Governor Claiborne informed the Spaniard that "the departure from the territory of yourself and ones attached to your department will be expected in the course of the present month." The month ended without Casa Calvo's departure. In February, Claiborne stated that his presence was unacceptable and sent him a passport. Under protest, Casa Calvo used the passport to repair to Havana, evidently leaving behind him unfulfilled schemes of a Spanish insurrection against the cursed Americans.

SALCEDO
(1801–1803)

Don Juan Manuel de Salcedo was the last Spanish governor of Louisiana. When he was appointed to the office in 1801, Louisiana had already been retroceded to France in the Treaty of San Ildefonso, but it was November 30, 1803, before French envoy Laussat arrived in New Orleans to take possession of it. Salcedo's governorship was a holding action until the French arrival.

For twenty days, France held Louisiana; then she transferred it to the United States; Claiborne and Wilkinson, the American commissioners, received it.

FOLCH
(1803–1811)

With the loss of the capital city of New Orleans, Spanish Alabama had to look to Pensacola as its new capital. Pensacola was only half the size of Mobile, but it became the residence of the new governor, Vincent Folch. According to P. J. Hamilton in *Colonial Mobile*, "from there now issued all regulations about land as well as political matters."

Folch had become the West Florida governor stationed in Pensacola in 1796 and served in that office for fifteen years. He had little influence over affairs in Mobile until after the Louisiana cession. However in the early, brighter days of Spanish rule, Folch, a captain in the Spanish army, had served as commandant in Mobile (from June 22, 1787, to March 30, 1792). As governor, Folch found that rule had eroded to a tenuous hold.

Internal troubles for Folch centered on the intendent Morales, who was a bitter political enemy. Morales' intrigues and political ploys threatened but did not topple Governor Folch.

More threatening and more dangerous were the Americans. In 1810, a group of insurgent Americans living in the Spanish district of Baton Rouge engineered a successful coup and captured the town. They proclaimed Baton Rouge and all Spanish territory east to the Perdido River as belonging to their new "Republic of West Florida." They ran up their flag, a white star on a field of blue wool, lodged complaints against the Spaniards, and requested President Madison to annex their "republic" to the United States.

President Madison ignored the new republic and the request for annexation. Instead, he issued a proclamation October 27, 1810, stating that the territory from the Mississippi to the Perdido had been part of the Louisiana Purchase. Simultaneously, Secretary of State Monroe issued orders for Governor Claiborne to occupy the Baton Rouge District and bring it under the government of the Orleans Territory.

Fulwar Skipworth, the insurgent governor, retreated into the Baton Rouge fort. Governor Claiborne's troops thereupon took the fort without bombardment and the "Republic of West Florida" came to a swift, inglorious end.

Meanwhile, in the Mobile district a group of revolutionaries from the Bigbee District, led by Reuben Kemper, were plotting to overthrow the Spanish in Mobile. They got as far as the Tensaw River, where they were captured by Spanish soldiers who then debarked them to Morro Castle prison in Havana.

Governor Folch on December 2, 1810, indicated in a letter to Indian agent John McKee that he was ready to surrender West Florida to American occupation if Spanish reinforcements were not on hand by January 1, 1811. This message was relayed to President Madison who immediately responded. However, it turned out Folch had changed his mind by the time any negotiations could begin.

Folch was succeeded in the office of West Florida governor by Francisco St. Maxent in 1811.

ST. MAXENT
(1811–1812)

Francisco Maximiliano de Saint Maxent was twice commandant of Mobile. His first tenure was from July 16, 1805, to August 30, 1807; his second was from March 22, 1805, to March 23, 1811. Apparently, he became governor or acting governor of West Florida after leaving his post as commandant at Mobile the second time. He served as governor for only a year. Within that year, the commandants in Mobile were changed eight times, a strong indication of the instability of the Spanish military structure there.

The Spanish must have known it was just a question of time before the Americans took Mobile, for Congress had already authorized President Madison to take possession of West Florida, employing the army and navy if needed. Yet, that possession did not take place for another year.

The Spanish Floridas could expect little support from the mother country, for the dynastic war between Ferdinand and Joseph Bonaparte was going on, and civil war was imminent. England and France were at war, and Spain's allegiance was wavering between an old friend, France, and England. In many ways, the Floridas were more of a burden to Spain now than an asset.

Meanwhile, in the Mobile District, the status of the citizens was also in abeyance, especially that of Americans who had purchased land in the earlier days before such sales were discontinued. One such citizen was Josiah Blakely who took an oath of allegiance to the Spanish crown and bought three islands holding thousands of acres of land. He wrote to his niece in Connecticut: "The unfortunate dispute between the two nations has rendered it impossible for me to either sell or cultivate these lands. Were the Americans here, their value would soon be known. When I came to this place, it was supposed the United States would soon be in possession. . . . By this long delay, I have been disappointed."

Governor Francisco St. Maxent was succeeded by Mauricio Zúñiga in 1812.

ZÚÑIGA
(1812–1813)

The last Spanish governor of Alabama was Don Mauricio de Zúñiga.

In the War of 1812 between the United States and England, Spain allowed England to use the port of Mobile. This was the excuse awaited by America for a "justified" show of force against the Spaniards. General Wilkinson with troops from New Orleans captured Dauphin Island, thirty miles south of Mobile, in April, 1813.

He deployed boats in Mobile Bay and troops from Ft. Stoddert to isolate Mobile from any reinforcements from Pensacola.

Following the capture of Dauphin Island, Wilkinson marched north to Mobile. There Cayetano Perez was commandant; in Fort Carlota he had sixty men, sixty-two cannon and munitions, and no provisions. He surrendered Ft. Carlota and the post of Mobile to General Wilkinson on April 15, 1813 at 5:00 P.M. No shot was fired on either side.

At last, all of Alabama had come under American possession.

5

Mississippi Territory
(1799–1817)

WINTHROP SARGENT
(1799–1801)

The Mississippi Territory was formed by an act of Congress in 1798 and included all of what is now Alabama except the Mobile District, added in 1813, and a part of the northern area. The new territory was administered at first by a military commandant until President Adams appointed Winthrop Sargent as the first governor in 1799.

Although Governor Sargent appears to have been unpopular with the territorial settlers, largely because of his fee system for salaried public officials and his hard-nosed "impartial" enforcement of the law, he accomplished a great deal during his short term.

He divided the Natchez District into three counties: Adams and Pickering in the area later to become the State of Mississippi, and Washington County in what would later be Alabama. This enormous territorial county extended from the Pearl River east to the Chattahoochee River. Baldwin and Clarke counties were later formed from a part of the original Washington County. McIntosh Bluff became the county seat and, as such, was the first center of American government in the land which would become the State of Alabama in 1819.

The formation of Washington County in the east resulted in two separate and distant settlements, the Natchez in Mississippi and the Tombigbee in Alabama. The Natchez District was the more populous and dominated the territorial assembly, thus sparking the agitation for a separate Territory of Alabama—a matter which became increasingly divisive and critical until the establishment of that new Territory in 1817. The Tombigbee people felt a particular injustice in their dangerous exposure to Indian attack and lack of military defenses. Working to the advantage of the Tombigbee settlers' hopes was the interest which slave state representatives in Congress had in adding another slave state to the Union.

There was considerable bickering back and forth over the years. When a division was finally decided upon, a compromise dividing line was accepted running from the Gulf north to the northwestern corner of Washington County, thence north to the entry of Bear Creek into the Tennessee River. This line in slightly altered form became the permanent western boundary of Alabama.

Governor Sargent, together with three judges, wrote and instituted the first Territorial Code of Law. In 1799, Fort Stoddert was erected fifty miles north of Mobile as protection against the Indians and to guard St. Stephens. Sargent, everything considered, was an able and conscientious administrator.

Winthrop Sargent was born on May 1, 1753 at Gloucester, Massachusetts, the son of Winthrop and Judith Sanders Sargent. He graduated from Harvard in 1771; at the outbreak of the Revolutionary War, he enlisted in the Continental Army and served to the rank of major. In 1787, Sargent was appointed secretary to the governor of the territory northwest of the Ohio River and later became acting governor. In 1791, he was adjutant to Governor St. Clair in the expedition against the Indians and was twice wounded.

On February 9, 1789, Sargent married Rowena Tupper. After her death, he married Mary McIntosh Williams on October 4, 1798. President Jefferson, elected on the Republican party ticket (later the Democratic party) refused to reappoint Sargent (a Federalist) to the governorship and chose instead his friend William Claiborne. Sargent then retired to the plantation of his second wife to live out his years. He died aboard a Mississippi steamboat out of New Orleans on January 3, 1820.

Sargent was a scholar and member of the American Philosophical Society, the American Academy of Arts and Sciences, and the Massachusetts Historical Society. He contributed several articles to the scholarly periodicals of the time.

WILLIAM CLAIBORNE
(1801–1805)

William Charles Coles Claiborne, a native of Virginia, was a well-educated lawyer of high repute and former judge of the Tennessee Supreme Court. This affable and trusting gentleman was thrust into the frontier problems by his appointment as the second governor of the Mississippi Territory in 1801. He was appointed by his friend President Thomas Jefferson, first as Mississippi Territory governor, then as governor-general of the newly acquired Louisiana Territory in 1803, and finally as governor of the Orleans Province after the territory was divided in March, 1805. At this time, he relinquished his office as Mississippi Territory governor and was succeeded by Robert Williams.

Three forces worked to Claiborne's disadvantage in office—the duplicity of General Wilkinson, later proved a traitor, with whom the governor innocently cooperated; the hostility of the New Orleans Creoles who resented him as an outsider, preferring French rule; and the strong disapproval of the implacable and impetuous Andrew Jackson, who openly discredited Claiborne's defense measures for the District of Baton Rouge, which the governor had earlier seized from the Spanish on orders of President Madison. The complex problems attendant on this latter defense were innumerable, and when the defenses were overrun in the War of 1812 Claiborne was blamed. Yet, the British were later repulsed. After the American victory under Jackson at New Orleans, Claiborne's reputation seems to have revived, as his subsequent elections to high office attest.

David P. Mason, in his manuscript *Caladonian Indians in Southeast Alabama, 1790–1815,* notes that Claiborne "used almost his entire fortune to arm, feed and pay troops he used during the Creek War and later at the Battle of New Orleans. He was never reimbursed by the Federal government or by the people he fought to defend. The war also took his health. In a real sense, he gave his all for his country and people."

Governor Claiborne was born in 1775 in Sussex County, Virginia, son of William and Mary Leigh Claiborne. He studied at Richmond Academy and William and Mary College. At the age of sixteen, he left for the nation's capital in New York where he became a clerk of the Congress. With the encouragement of John Sevier, later governor of Tennessee, Claiborne returned to Virginia to study law. Shortly after being admitted to the bar, he moved to Sullivan County, Tennessee, where he began his law practice and gained a wide reputation in criminal practice. Claiborne was a delegate to the Ten-

Winthrop Sargent
1799–1801

William Charles Cole Claiborne
1801–1805

Robert Williams
1805–1809

David Holmes
1809–1817

nessee Constitutional Convention in 1796 and was later appointed a judge of the supreme court of the new state. In August, 1797, he was elected to fill out the congressional term of Andrew Jackson and was reelected in 1799.

When President Jefferson appointed him governor of the new Mississippi Territory in July of 1800, Claiborne was twenty-six years of age. His administration seems to have been popular and efficient. During his tenure, a delegate was selected to represent the territory in the U.S. House of Representatives; the capital was moved from Natchez to Washington, six miles east. A committee was appointed by Congress to settle disputed land titles, and a territorial militia was organized. The boundary of the territory was extended north to the Tennessee line on lands acquired following the territorial settlement with South Carolina and Georgia.

In November, 1803, Claiborne was appointed with General Wilkinson as a commissioner to accept the transfer of the newly purchased Louisiana Territory, and his long involvement with the Louisiana area began. When Louisiana became a state in 1812, Claiborne was elected the first governor, occupying that position until December, 1816.

In January, 1817, Claiborne was elected to the U.S. Senate, but unfortunately he saw no service in that body. He became ill shortly after the election and died in New Orleans on November 23, 1817, at the age of forty-two.

Claiborne was married three times. His first wife was Eliza W. Lewis of Nashville, who died in 1804; the second was Clarissa Duralde and the third, Suzette Bosque. The latter two were both of prominent New Orleans Creole families, and the marriage alliances did much to alleviate the difficulties of the governor's office.

At his death, Claiborne was universally mourned. His reputation as a leader of ability and integrity in an impossibly difficult period seems assured. What he lacked in force he had compensated for in part by his diligence, generosity, and affability.

ROBERT WILLIAMS
(1805–1809)

On March 1, 1805, President Jefferson appointed Robert Williams governor of the Mississippi Territory to succeed Claiborne. Williams held this office until his resignation in March, 1809.

An able lawyer with considerable legislative service in the North Carolina state senate (1792–1795) and the U.S. House of Representatives (1797–1802), he was well equipped to administer the affairs of the territory.

In 1805, a federal post office was established at St. Stephens, and the town was incorporated in 1807. Subsequently, a federal trading post was set up there and Washington Academy established. By proclamation of Governor Williams, the second Alabama county, Madison, was created on December 13, 1808, and the county seat fixed at Huntsville. Huntsville was incorporated in 1811 and became one of the important political, social, and commercial centers of the state. Settlement of Coffeeville was begun in 1808.

An exciting occurrence of the period was the capture of Aaron Burr near St. Stephens. Burr had escaped after his arrest at Natchez and was traveling in disguise to Spanish Mobile. A $2,000 reward was offered by Williams for capture of Burr. Local resident Nicholas Perkins recognized Burr and notified Lt. Edward P. Gaines, commandant of Ft. Stoddert, who arrested him and arranged his transfer to Richmond, Virginia, where Burr was tried and acquitted in a memorable U.S. court proceeding.

Robert Williams was born in Prince Edward County, Virginia in 1768, the son of Nathaniel and Mary Ann Williamson Williams. The family settled in North Carolina where Robert studied law and later set up a practice in Nottingham County. After his service in the state senate and the U.S. Congress, Williams was appointed in 1803 a commissioner, with Thomas Rodney, to settle land claims in the Mississippi Territory west of the Pearl River. In 1805, Williams became the Territorial Governor.

Governor Williams was married to Elizabeth Winston of North Carolina, who died near Washington, Mississippi Territory, in 1814. In his later life, Governor Williams became a planter in Ouachita Parish, Louisiana, where he died on January 25, 1836.

DAVID HOLMES
(1809–1817)

David Holmes was the last of the Mississippi territorial governors and served the longest. The territory grew rapidly during his successive terms, terminating in the statehood of Mississippi and the election of Holmes as its first governor. Two wars marked Holmes' term—the Creek Indian War (most of the fighting in the Alabama area to the east) and the War of 1812, which included the important seizure of the Mobile District from the Spanish and which terminated in the dramatic victory over the British at New Orleans.

From the beginning of Holmes' governorship, the territory was threatened by hostile Creeks and Chickasaws, and there was great animosity growing among the Americans toward the Spanish in West Florida and the Mobile District. Holmes' difficulty in the beginning was to restrain his people from attacking the Spanish. He ordered the troops at Ft. Stoddert to provide protection for the Spanish at Mobile. However, at the appropriate time, he cooperated with Governor Claiborne of Louisiana in seizing the Spanish District of Baton Rouge, and after President Madison's order to take Mobile he cooperated with General Wilkinson in this campaign. The Spanish commandant, Cayetano Perez, seeing his garrison vastly outnumbered, surrendered without a fight on April 15, 1813, and Mobile, the birthplace of European settlement in southeastern America, came under the flag of the United States at last.

In 1816, the territory was enlarged by cessions of land from the Choctaws and Chickasaws. In 1817, the territory was divided, Mississippi becoming a state, the area to the east becoming the Alabama Territory.

Holmes was delegate to and president of the Mississippi Constitutional Convention of 1817 and served as first Mississippi state governor until January, 1820. In August of that same year, he was appointed to the U.S. Senate, later elected to that office, and served until September, 1825, when he resigned. He again won the governorship in 1825 and was inaugurated in January, 1826; but his health soon failed, and he resigned in July of that year to retire to his old home in Virginia.

David Holmes was a native of York County, Pennsylvania. He was born March 10, 1770, son of Joseph and Rebecca Hunter Holmes. He grew up in Frederick County, Virginia, where his father was a merchant. David attended the boys' academy in Winchester, Virginia, and in 1790 began the study of law in Williamsburg. After being admitted to the bar, he set up practice in Harrisonburg and was made commonwealth attorney for Rockingham County. He ran as a Jeffersonian Republican for the U.S. Congress in 1797, was elected, and served six consecutive terms. His service in the Congress terminated when he accepted the appointment as governor of the Mississippi Territory in 1809.

Holmes suffered a prolonged illness following his retirement to Virginia and died on August 20, 1832, at the age of sixty-two. He was never married.

Alabama Territory

WILLIAM BIBB
(1817–1819)

(See State of Alabama Governors)

6

State of Alabama
(1819–1974)

Alabama had at last become an identity in itself, first as
a territory, then as a state. The long colonial period was
past; the Indian threat had been disposed of; the Spanish
in the Mobile District had finally been washed out of the
hair of the new republic. Following statehood for Mississippi and the formation of the Alabama Territory, rapid
increase in population took place. Alabama was admitted
to the Union as a state in 1819.

WILLIAM WYATT BIBB
(November, 1819–July, 1820)
Autauga County

The man who presided over Alabama as governor
during the transition period from territory to statehood
and during the formative period of the new state was
William Wyatt Bibb. The fact that he served less than a
year as governor of the state does not attenuate the deep
influence of his work as young Alabama grappled with
the problems of its birth and cradle days. Bibb was the
only governor of the Alabama Territory and the first

governor of the state, serving until his death on July 10, 1820, the result of a fall from a horse.

This remarkable man, like many other political leaders of the South at this time, was a native of Virginia. He was born October 2, 1781, at Amelia City, Prince Edward County, Virginia, the eldest son of Captain William Bibb, a Revolutionary War hero, and Sally Wyatt Bibb, descendant of former governor Francis Wyatt of Virginia.

The family moved to Elbert County, Georgia, where Captain Bibb died in 1796, leaving a widow and eight children. Even under trying circumstances, Mrs. Bibb managed to send her eldest son to college. He attended William and Mary and later the medical college of the University of Pennsylvania, where he received his M.D. in 1801.

Dr. Bibb set up medical practice in Petersburg, Georgia. In 1803 he married Mary Freeman, daughter of Colonel Holman Freeman, also of Revolutionary War fame.

But the call of politics must have been irresistible in those early days of the republic. At age twenty-one, Dr. Bibb ran for and was elected to the Georgia house of representatives and later to the state senate. After four years in the legislature, he was elected to the U.S. Congress where he served from 1806 to 1813. He was appointed that same year to fill the senatorial vacancy created by the resignation of William H. Crawford and served in the Senate to the expiration of that term. He ran for reelection in 1816; being defeated by George M. Troup, Bibb resigned before his term expired.

Only a few months later, in April, 1817, President Monroe appointed Bibb governor of the newly formed Territory of Alabama. Within days, Bibb was at his duties in St. Stephens, Alabama, the territorial capital on the banks of the Tombigbee River. The first territorial legislative session met January 19, 1818, and the thirteen members elected Gabriel Moore of Huntsville as speaker.

The upper house was then called the council. According to the terms of the new state charter, the old three-man Mississippi Council was to preside, temporarily, in the Alabama Territory.

However, when the council met, one member had died and one had resigned, leaving only one representative, James Titus. According to Summersell's *Alabama History,* "Titus called the council to order, answered the roll call, organized the council, elected himself president of the council . . . voted on bills, and declared for adjournment."

Governor Bibb's message to the legislature was concerned mainly with education and internal development, primarily transportation. New banks were chartered and thirteen new counties were formed.

At the second session in December, 1818, the legislature petitioned the U.S. Congress for admission of Alabama to statehood. They also selected, at Bibb's direction, a tract of land at the confluence of the Cahaba and Alabama rivers in southcentral Alabama as the site of the new capital, and Governor Bibb was commissioned to "lay off the town of Cahaba on this site."

The Alabama Constitutional Convention of 1819 met July 9 at Huntsville in populous Madison County to draft and adopt a new constitution. Some of the most distinguished men of that period had assembled in Huntsville. John W. Walker, a native Virginian, was elected president of the convention, and a committee of fifteen was appointed by him to draft the constitution. It was very similar to that of Mississippi, providing for executive, judicial, and legislative departments, and included a bill of rights modeled on that of the U.S. Constitution.

In the first gubernatorial election, William Wyatt Bibb ran against Marmaduke Williams of Tuscaloosa, a former Congressman from North Carolina. In this contest, political factions developed which were to become known as the Georgia faction, of which Bibb was a member, and the North Carolina faction, later to become a power under Israel Pickens. Also, the long continuing political conflict between northern and southern Alabama first stirred itself in this election. The issues were the location of the capital and the type of county representation in the legislature, that is, either a prescribed number from each county or a proportionate representation according to population. The north, with populous Madison County, wanted proportionate and the south wanted prescribed representation. A compromise was reached with the south accepting proportionate representation in turn for having the capital located at Cahaba. The temporary capital was to be Huntsville. Bibb won the race for governor by 1,202 votes out of a total of 15,482.

Bibb's message to the first legislature reemphasized the need to set up schools and other institutions of education and to begin building urgently needed roads and developing water transportation. Actually, the great steamboat era on Alabama's rivers was about to begin.

During this period of Bibb's tenure, General Andrew Jackson, hero of the Creek Indian wars which had cleared Alabama for settlers, visited Huntsville and was lauded by the legislature and lionized by the public. But there were some who opposed him—the planters, the rich aristocracy (what there was of it)—and Bibb was among them. This cleavage in attitudes toward the general led to the formation of powerful political machines, out of the camps of the already established North Carolina and Georgia factions. Crawford's Georgia machine, which included Governor Bibb, stood opposed to the Jack-sonian democracy, supporting in a sense a semi-oligarchy of the educated, the rich, and influential. The North Carolinians under Israel Pickens, supporters of Jackson and Jacksonian democracy, spoke for the plain people. This party was destined to break the back of the Georgians following the death of Governor Bibb in July, 1820.

THOMAS BIBB
(July, 1820–November, 1821)
Limestone County

Thomas Bibb, younger brother of Governor William Wyatt Bibb, was a college-educated planter, merchant, and law-maker, who came into the governor's chair via the legislative route upon the death of his brother. He was at the time president of the senate, and he automatically became Alabama's second governor. His brother had served less than a year, and Thomas, who served out the remaining term of approximately a year and a half, did not run for reelection. Between the two brothers, the first full term of the governorship of Alabama was filled.

Thomas was governor when the capital was moved from Huntsville to Cahaba in 1820; the legislature assembled in the new capitol building on November 6 of that year. The younger Bibb continued his brother's spade work in laying the foundation of a new state government, but nothing dramatic occurred during this relatively peaceful time—if one excepts the beginnings of the bank controversy during which Thomas Bibb, favorable to the interests of the private banks, ran head on into Israel Pickens, who later established the state bank. Thomas was to become a director of the Huntsville bank in which the controversy over banking methods and the "interest of the people" had originally arisen.

Thomas was born in Virginia in 1784 but grew up in Georgia. He moved to Madison County, Alabama in 1816. Here he met his bride-to-be, Parmelia Thompson, daughter of Robert and Sarah Thompson, native Virginians. Belle Mina near Huntsville, one of Alabama's great antebellum mansions, was their home. Thomas became one of the pioneer settlers of Limestone County, moving there shortly after the territory was purchased from the Indians.

Bibb represented Limestone in the Constitutional Convention of 1819 and, in that same year, was elected to the state senate. He was duly elected presiding officer of that body and from there, upon the death of his brother, came to the governorship.

Although Thomas Bibb did not run for a second term as governor, he did not retire entirely from politics. He once more represented Limestone County in the state legislature and was also a member of the state convention of 1825, formed to amend the original constitution of 1819.

Thomas Bibb died in 1838 at the age of fifty-four.

ISRAEL PICKENS
(1821–1825)
Greene County

With Israel Pickens, native North Carolinian, resident of Washington County and later of Greene County,* may be dated the beginning of definite political alliances and vigorous political battles in Alabama. Pick-

---

*That part of Greene County in which Pickens lived later became a part of Hale County.

ens was the first to serve a full term as governor. He served two terms, in fact, and turned the political tide against the Georgia machine, which had supported his two predecessors and had come to represent, in the eyes of the average voter, the interests of the aristocratic, the monied, and the powerful.

Paradoxically, Pickens himself was a man of aristocratic background, well educated, and not entirely outside the circle of monied interests, having served as president of the Tombecbe Bank and as an officer of the Bank of Mobile, founded in 1818. But following the depression of 1819, he apparently saw the need for a state bank, as a government-controlled assist to the people who had lost money and had little credit left. Again, paradoxically, although he and Andrew Jackson (a figure of growing political dominance in Alabama at this time) seemed in perfect accord concerning the interests of the common man, they differed on the banking question. Jackson opposed the state-owned bank.

However, when Pickens ran for a second term, the banking issue was paramount, virtually the only issue; and upon his election, the bank was established. With the second defeat of his opponent—Dr. Henry Chambers of Madison County, candidate of the Georgia machine— the power of that machine and its leader, Crawford, was broken. Even at this early stage in Alabama history, the old division of interests between the haves and the have-nots asserted itself, and the spokesman for the have-nots was Israel Pickens, Alabama's third governor.

Born January 30, 1780, near Concord, North Carolina, he was the son of Samuel and Jane Pickens, the former a Revolutionary soldier. Young Pickens had unusually good education for the time in the private schools of Iredell County, North Carolina, and he attended Jefferson College in Canonsburg, Pennsylvania, graduating in 1802. He read law and was shortly after admitted to the North Carolina bar in Burke County, North Carolina.

Pickens served in the upper house of the North Carolina legislature, 1808–1809, and in the U.S. House of Representatives, 1811–1817. He was married in June, 1814, to Martha Orille Lenoir of North Carolina.

After leaving Congress, Pickens was appointed land register for the new territory of Alabama and took up his duties at St. Stephens, Alabama in 1817. He was soon to represent Washington County in the convention which framed the first constitution for his new state. He later moved to Greene County where he was resident when elected governor.

Pickens was the power who formed the only political group which opposed the Georgians. In the campaign of 1821, his opponent was Dr. Chambers, supporter of private banks and choice of the Georgia machine. Pickens was elected governor by a vote of 9,114 to 7,129.

The State Banking Act of 1821 was passed by his legislature, yet Pickens vetoed it because it gave virtual control of banks to the various private banking interests. In the gubernatorial race of 1823, when he was again opposed by Chambers, the banking issue was still paramount and Pickens won, this time by a vote of 6,942 to 4,604. He indeed had a mandate, and the kind of charter he wanted for the state bank was drawn up. The bank opened its doors in Cahaba in July of 1824. The bank's capital amounted to more than $200,000; its mission was the relief of impoverished landowners and farmers.

The University of Alabama was established during Pickens' administration (although it did not open its doors until 1831), and he became the first ex-officio president of its board.

Pickens was considered an able administrator, and during his two terms the foundation of the new state government was largely formulated and set in motion. The town of Greensboro was incorporated, and Pike, Covington, Dale, Fayette, and Walker counties were created.

An interesting aside in the career of this man was his active part in the American Colonization Society, a group also supported by Presidents James Monroe and James Madison. The mission of the society was to free the slaves and provide a colony in Africa to which they could return as free men. The Alabama Colonization Society was a branch of the parent organization and Israel Pickens was its president. A later governor, John Gayle, was also active in the society. Before its ultimate failure, the organization founded the colony of Liberia on Africa's west coast, and its capital was named Monrovia in honor of President James Monroe.

After his second term as governor, Pickens was appointed by his successor, John Murphy, to the U.S. Senate to fill the vacancy created by the death of Dr. Crawford, his old political enemy.

However, ill health overtook Pickens, and he left the Senate to retire to Cuba in an attempt to arrest his growing lung disease. He died there April 24, 1827. He is buried three miles south of Greensboro near his old home.

Pickens might easily be rated one of the more successful early governors. He was a man of exceptional capability, vision, and compassion.

JOHN MURPHY
(1825–1829)
Monroe County

The North Carolina faction was well entrenched by the time John Murphy, a native North Carolinian, was elected in 1825. He was hand picked by Pickens, and he ran without opposition, receiving a plurality vote of 12,500. He was reelected in 1827, again without opposition.

Murphy was, of course, solidly behind the state bank; and aside from the beginnings of the controversy concerning removal of the Indians from their territories in Alabama, no local issues of exciting import evolved in his two administrations. The capital had to be moved from Cahaba to Tuscaloosa, but this was due to an act of God, not Murphy. Damaging floods occurred so heavily in 1825 that the Alabama legislature had to be transported to the second story of the capitol building in rowboats to make their entry through windows. The capital was moved in 1826 to Tuscaloosa, but Cahaba continued as a thriving cultural and economic center for Black Belt Alabama until the end of the Civil War.

The stirring issues of the time were national, and the most crucial of these was the protective tariff dubbed "The Tariff of Abominations" in 1828. There was strong opposition to it in the South, and Murphy denounced it in a speech to the legislature as "unconstitutional." However, when the lines were drawn tight by South Carolina's Nullification Act, Governor Murphy supported President Jackson in his aggressive moves to bring South Carolina to heel and keep the Union together.

Following his two terms in the governor's chair, Murphy went home to his plantation in Clarke County; but he soon reentered politics on the congressional scene. He was defeated once in his bid for Congress, then elected in 1833 over Judge James Dellett. A subsequent attempt saw his defeat in 1839 after which he retired to his plantation where he lived the remainder of his life.

William Wyatt Bibb
March, 1817–November, 1819
November, 1819–July, 1820

Thomas Bibb
1820–1821

Israel Pickens
1821–1825

John Murphy
1825–1829

John Murphy was born in 1785 in Robeson County, North Carolina, son of Neil Murphy, a Scottish immigrant. The governor's brother was Reverend Murdock Murphy, first pastor of the Government Street Presbyterian Church of Mobile.

When only a child, John moved with his family to South Carolina, where he later taught school to earn money for college. He entered South Carolina College, where he was a classmate of John Gayle, a later Alabama governor. Graduating in 1808, Murphy entered upon the study of law. He was made clerk of the South Carolina senate and held this post for ten years, a time in which he undoubtedly gained much insight into the politics and politicians of the time. He was also made a trustee of the University of South Carolina, 1809–1818.

He moved to Alabama (still a territory) in 1818, settling in Monroe County. He was admitted to the bar there but spent his time supervising his plantation until the call of state duties and political contest drew him back into public life.

He was a member of the Alabama Constitutional Convention of 1819, was elected to the state legislature in 1820, the state Senate in 1822, and to the governorship in 1825.

He was twice married, first to Sarah Hails of South Carolina, next to a Mrs. Carter of Clarke County. Historian W. Brewer describes Governor Murphy as "stout, unwieldy . . . [his] temperament was phlegmatic . . . [he was] practical, but not at all brilliant . . . pious and benevolent and honorable both in private and public affairs." His was not an exciting tenure as governor, but it was solid.

After two years of retirement from an active public service, Governor Murphy died on his beloved plantation on September 21, 1841.

GABRIEL MOORE
(1829–March, 1831)
Madison County

Gabriel Moore was quite the opposite of his predecessor in office. John Murphy was as colorful as eroded
sandstone. Gabriel Moore was handsome and hot-
tempered, a man who drank when he liked, frequently
with his constituents. He was married once, under conditions never made clear, and almost immediately ob-
tained a divorce, only to follow this by a pistol duel with
his ex-bride's brother, an encounter in which the brother
was wounded.

Such was the man who followed the stodgy Murphy
and who made the welkin ring with excitement in young
Alabama. Moore was eminently qualified for the office of
governor.

Born in 1785 in Stokes County, North Carolina, Gabriel was the son of Matthew and Letitia Dalton Moore
and grandson of John Moore of Albemarle County, Virginia. Gabriel Moore was one of the earliest settlers of
Madison County, Alabama when it was still part of the
Mississippi Territory. He settled in Huntsville in 1810
and took up his law practice there; he represented the
county in the territorial legislature, continued in that
office under the Alabama Territory (1817), and was chosen speaker of the lower house.

In 1821, he was elected to the Congress of the United
States, and beat a strong opponent and future governor
of Alabama, Clement Comer Clay, in the election of
1827. He held his seat in the Congress until he was
elected governor of Alabama in 1829, running without
opposition, as most strong Jackson supporters were apt
to do in those Jackson years.

As governor, Moore disliked but complied with the federal protective tariff acts and advised the people to use "ordinary means of redress under the constitution." In his bold fight against the nullification matter, he spoke out with candor. He also proposed that the Alabama delegation in Congress be instructed to vote against the recharter of the Bank of the United States.

He was deeply interested in the construction of the Tennessee River canal which bypassed the Muscle Shoals construction to make the river navigable across all northern Alabama. He saw in his term the opening of the doors of the University of Alabama at Tuscaloosa, an institution he supported. Spring Hill College in Mobile also came into existence in 1831 under the supervision of the Jesuits. Moore advocated the establishment of a state penitentiary and revision of the penal code.

The county of Lowndes was created in Moore's administration, and the Treaty of Dancing Rabbit Creek was effected. In the latter agreement, the Choctaw Indians, who had fought alongside the Americans in the Creek Indian Wars, gave up all the land remaining to them in Alabama.

The census of 1830 showed a population of 309,527, almost double that of 1820—Alabama was growing like an adolescent farm boy. The first state railroad was chartered at this time, running a total distance of about four miles from Tuscumbia to Sheffield.

During his last year as governor, Moore was elected to the U.S. Senate over John McKinley of Lauderdale County. The state senate voted 49 to 40 for Moore. Resigning as governor, he entered the Senate March 4, 1831, and served for six years.

In 1832, Moore voted to reject Martin Van Buren as minister to Great Britain, an act of heresy which ended his friendship with Jackson and brought the wrath of his constituency in Alabama down upon him. The state legislature requested his resignation from the U.S. Senate, a favor which he did not confer upon them. Nevertheless, Moore's political power was doomed, and in the senatorial contest of 1837 against Reuben Chapman (another future Alabama governor), Gabriel Moore met his first defeat. In 1843, he moved to Texas where he died two years later.

SAMUEL B. MOORE
(March, 1831–November, 1831)
Jackson County

Samuel Moore succeeded to the governorship from his post as president of the state senate. When Gabriel Moore resigned the governorship to take his seat in the U.S. Senate in March, 1831, Samuel Moore moved automatically into the governor's chair.

He served nine months; though he ran for reelection, he was defeated by the formidable John Gayle of Greene County. Another opponent, Nicholas Davis, a wealthy planter and Whig from Limestone County, was also defeated by Gayle.

Samuel Moore was ardent in his support of the state bank and in a speech to the legislature urged caution "in procuring ability and integrity in [the bank's] direction." He was also opposed to nullification. However, there was little time in his short tenure for Samuel Moore to demonstrate his abilities as first officer of the state.

Moore came from Franklin County, Tennessee, where he was born in 1789, moving to Jackson County, Alabama as a child. Beginning in 1823, he represented that county in the legislature, moving up to the state senate in 1828. After his defeat in the governor's race of

1831, Moore returned to his residence in Pickens County, represented that county in the state senate 1834–1838, and was again elected president of that body in 1835. He also served as judge of the Pickens County court 1835–1841.

Samuel Moore died in Carrollton, Alabama on November 7, 1846, still a bachelor.

JOHN GAYLE
(1831–1835)
Greene County

John Gayle's two terms as governor were filled with conflict. During his tenure, for the first time the issue of states' rights vs federal authority became prominent. Gayle was an ardent states' rights man and, as governor, fought the federal government to a standstill on the question, thereby losing the close ties he had held with Andrew Jackson.

Although a planter, Gayle was allied strongly for many years with the Democratic party and thus opposed the rising Whig party, composed of planters from the Black Belt and the rich Tennessee Valley. Except for the Tennessee Valley, the division was almost totally one between southern and northern Alabama. Politically, Gayle represented the common man and was a stout supporter of Jacksonian democracy.

When Dixon Lewis of Montgomery County advocated nullification, Gayle attacked him and became overnight one of the most eloquent spokesmen against this doctrine. Nullification became one of the large issues in the campaign of 1831, and Gayle stood closely allied with the old hero Jackson in opposing it. After he won the election, Gayle's first address to the general assembly was a ringing denunciation of nullification and a masterpiece of defense of the Union undivided.

Jackson was, perhaps, at the height of his popularity and political power in Alabama when he ran for reelection to the presidency in 1832. It was almost impossible to defeat any political candidate in Alabama who had the solid backing of Andrew Jackson.

Then came one of those ironies which separated the two men permanently—in this case the problem of Indian removal. Jackson had become a legendary hero in Alabama principally because he had defeated and broken the power of the Creek tribes, an act which eventually opened up the lands of what was to become Alabama to thousands of white settlers. In the treaty which resulted in the Indian Removal Act by Congress, the Indian nations gave up all their territory in Alabama. The same treaty stipulated, however, that individual Indians might remain on ceded land until such time as surveys were completed and Indian selections were made. The federal law strictly forbade any moving in of "white intruders" in an effort to force out such individual Indian families. Hundreds of settlers ignored the law and moved indiscriminately onto Indian land. A crisis resulted when, in August, 1832, U.S. marshalls and federal troops from Fort Mitchell attempted to drive out the white squatters.

Governor Gayle took an uncompromising stand with the white settlers against the federal force. He made it clear that he believed the state itself had priority in any "right of negotiation" on any treaty dealing with land within the territory of that state. And he stated "the courts should adjudicate the conflict." While cautioning calm, he organized the militia in the new counties formed from the Indian territory.

Standing firm for states' rights and in opposition to the old hero Jackson, Gayle incredibly was swept back into office in 1832. Although he was severely criticized by many newspapers and some political leaders, Gayle was unopposed for the governorship.

Gayle appealed the settlers' claim to Washington and submitted his case to the state legislature. He termed the government's policy "an unconstitutional interference with our local and internal affairs, and as a measure of revolting injustice and oppression toward that portion of our inhabitants who have not injured the Indians." The ugly specter of a constitutional challenge, which would all too soon lead to Civil War, had raised its head to perplex the young nation.

Fortunately, Alabama's congressional delegation in Washington—men such as William R. King, Gabriel Moore, Clement C. Clay, John Murphy, and Dixon Lewis —were able to lay the ground for compromise. They convinced Jackson to send Francis Scott Key to the Alabama capital at Tuscaloosa to negotiate. In the end, Key conceded virtually everything that Gayle wanted.

This crisis not only broke the strong friendship between Gayle and Jackson and attenuated Jackson's popularity in the state, but it led to a realignment of political parties in Alabama—states' rightists vs Unionists in both the Whig and Democratic parties. Gayle shortly thereafter joined the Whig party, aligning with the states' rights faction, and attempted to defeat Senator King, a Unionist, for the senatorial seat. He failed.

In the election of 1835, the Jackson Democrats elected Judge Clement C. Clay governor over Enoch Parsons of Monroe County, a planter and states' rights candidate of the Whigs. But in the next presidential election these same Unionists (along with the states' righters) supported Judge Hugh White of Tennessee to run against Jackson's choice, Martin Van Buren. Van Buren carried the state by a small majority of 4,894. Apparently, old political alignments were split along several lines, but the states' rights vs Union issue dominated all else.

Governor Gayle strongly supported the state bank and believed it might in time relieve people of much taxation. But, in fact, Alabama was moving toward a financial depression which would take the state bank down with it. However, for the time, the financial bubble was expanding, stimulated by speculation, sale of slaves, issuance of more and more paper money, and overextended loans.

But it was not all political in-fighting with Gayle. He advocated a railroad to be constructed from Courtland on the Tennessee River to Jackson on the Tombigbee to offset the transportation barrier of the Muscle Shoals on the Tennessee. The canal around the shoals was completed in 1836, but was not workable at all levels of the river and was abandoned in 1837. A railroad of forty-four miles length was built from Tuscumbia to Decatur, circumventing the shoals. Gayle also proposed a Tennessee–Tombigbee Canal to join Fort Deposit on the Tennessee to Tuscaloosa on the Black Warrior River —the first proposal anticipating the Tenn–Tom canal which would be under construction 134 years later. Nine new counties were created during his administration: Randolph, Talladega, Chambers, Tallapoosa, Coosa, Russell, Macon, Barbour, and Sumter. The towns of Livingston, Gainsville, Clayton (then county seat of Baldwin), Marion, and Autaugaville were established. The Bell factory at Huntsville, Alabama's first textile plant, was built, and Daniel Pratt set up the first plant for the manufacture of the cotton gin at Prattville.

John Gayle was born in Sumter District, North Carolina on September 11, 1792, son of Matthew and Mary Reese Gayle. He was educated at Newberry

Academy and South Carolina College, from which he graduated in 1813. That same year, he moved to Claiborne, Monroe County, Alabama and read law in the office of the Honorable A. S. Lipscomb. He was licensed to practice law in 1818. In the first session of the territorial legislature, Gayle was nominated to the territorial council. The legislature elected him solicitor of his circuit, an office he held for two years before resigning.

In 1822–1823, Gayle represented Monroe County in the state legislature; in 1823 he was chosen to succeed Judge Webb on the Alabama supreme court. He resigned this office the next year to represent Greene County in the legislature, where he was elected speaker of the house.

Gayle was elected governor in November, 1831, with a majority of 14,843 votes to 8,137 for Nicholas Davis, a Whig, and 3,643 for ex-governor Samuel Moore. He was reelected in 1833 without opposition.

Gayle was a presidential elector in 1836 and again in 1840. In 1847, he was elected to Congress where he served two terms before being appointed a federal district judge, an office he retained until his death July 21, 1859. He was a resident of Mobile in his later years, moving there to open a law practice at the end of his second term as governor.

Gayle, a member of the Presbyterian Church, was twice married—first, to Sarah Ann Haynsworth of Claiborne whom he wed in November, 1819, and then to Clarissa Stedman on November 1, 1839.

Governor Gayle was a man of generosity, deep compassion, and a high intelligence. As a dynamic leader of the people in these stirring early days, John Gayle created for himself a permanent seat among the giants.

CLEMENT COMER CLAY
(1835–July, 1837)
Madison County

Like a scene from an old frontier novel, a young Virginian and his Negro manservant, the young traveler's lawbooks stuffed in his saddlebags, rode one day into the new settlement of Huntsville, located in the Tennessee Valley between the green mountains and the broad, clear waters of the Tennessee River. It was the year 1811, eight years before Alabama became a state. The Creek Indians still ruled most of the territory, and nearly everything between Huntsville (population 4,000) and Mobile was a wilderness. The young newcomer, Clement Comer Clay, was destined to become state supreme court chief justice, U.S. senator, and governor of the new state of Alabama.

Although Clay was born into an old Virginia family, his was not the inheritance of wealth but rather of aristocracy of character and achievement and of superior intellect. Clay was born on December 17, 1789, in Halifax County, Virginia, the son of William Clay, a Revolutionary soldier, and Rebecca Comer Clay. At an early age, Clay moved with his family to Craiger County, Tennessee, where he continued his education until his graduation from East Tennessee College (later the University of Tennessee) in 1807. He read law under Hugh L. White of Knoxville and was admitted to the bar in 1809.

At his new home in Huntsville, Clay set up law practice, but had to abandon this temporarily while he joined Jackson's army in the fight against the Creeks in 1813. In the ranks he rose from private to adjutant. In 1815, Clay married Susanna Claiborne Withers.

Clay served as a member of the territorial legislature, 1817–1819, as a delegate to the Alabama Constitutional

Convention of 1819, and as chairman of the commission which drafted the first laws of the state and wrote its first constitution. As a circuit judge, he became a member of the provisional state supreme court in 1820 and was elected its chief justice. He resigned the bench in 1823 to resume his law practice, but the call of politics soon proved overwhelming.

Clay was a man with a high sense of honor and unfortunately very sensitive about it. He was involved in a duel in 1823 with Dr. Waddy Tate of Limestone County in which both men were wounded, but this did not keep him from the political arena.

He ran for the U.S. Congress against Gabriel Moore in 1827, but the canny Moore defeated Clay by cleverly identifying him, in the eyes of the average voter, with the rich aristocracy. However, Clay was elected to the state legislature that same year and became speaker of the lower house; in 1829 he was elected to the U.S. Congress where he served without opposition until 1835.

In the Congress, Clay was a member of the Alabama delegation which worked out the basis for a compromise on the Indian removal crisis occurring during Gayle's administration. He also was a firm Jackson man, supporting him in his attacks on the federal bank and in his opposition to nullification. However, Clay refused to vote for the Force Bill of March 2, 1833, which authorized Jackson to use the army and navy where necessary to collect unpopular customs duties. Fortunately, a compromise was worked out between Jackson and South Carolina Unionists which made use of the Force Act unnecessary.

Clay supported Van Buren, Jackson's choice for the presidency, against his old friend and tutor, Hugh L. White. White retaliated by supporting Enoch Parsons, a planter and states' rights Whig candidate, against Clay for the governorship in 1835. White's support for Parsons was not enough, however; Clay won by a vote of 23,297 to 12,209, the largest majority ever polled to that date.

In the spring of 1836, the Indian problem again stirred fears in the settlers of Alabama. The Creeks were threatening to go on the warpath and in some cases were raiding white settlers' homes. Again, the Indian action grew out of frustration with the white squatters' encroachment on territory still legally belonging to the Indians under the treaty of 1832. However, Governor Clay acted quickly to curtail violence by ordering Major General Patterson in northern Alabama and Brigadier General Moore of the Mobile district to converge with their troops on the scene of the uprising near Montgomery. Clay himself established a headquarters at Montgomery and was soon able to organize councils with some dozen chiefs and lay the foundation for a peaceful settlement.

Marshall, De Kalb, and Cherokee counties were created out of land ceded by the Cherokees in exchange for lands in the western United States, under the Treaty of New Echota. The Alabama and City of Montgomery Railroad was chartered, and for a time things looked prosperous, with the profits from the state bank meeting the governmental expenses and making direct taxes on the people unnecessary.

However, the halcyon days were numbered. In the spring of 1837, there was a run on the bank which then suspended specie payment, and a major financial crisis was on.

Clay called the legislature into extra session, and in his message to that body he recommended that the banks be continued, but under "proper restraints," especially regarding issuance of notes. The governor finally advised continuing the suspension of specie for a year to give the banks relief.

Clay, however, opposed the legislature's issuing public bonds in excess of $5 million. He ordered the bank's directors to make a detailed report, but apparently the records were so inadequate that no meaningful financial report could be made. Reckless management and overconfidence had carried the state banks beyond their means. At this point, Clay was appointed to the U.S. Senate. When Hugh McVay replaced Clay as governor in July, 1837, he stated that he believed the financial action of the legislature had done the job. However, the banks were doomed. It became the painful province of ex-Governor Clay in 1846 to act as a committeeman to wind up the affairs of the defunct state bank.

Clay served in the U.S. Senate from 1837 to 1841 when he resigned. As senator, he introduced a land graduation bill in 1838 designed to make millions of acres of valuable land available to citizens for purchase. His idea, in somewhat altered form, became law as the Benton Bill of 1854. He also supported the preemptive laws which gave original settlers who had lived on and improved the land a first right to purchase said land at the minimum price fixed by law.

When Senator Clay returned home, he was commissioned by the state legislature to prepare a digest of the laws of Alabama. He completed this task in 1843, and in this same year was again appointed to serve on the state supreme court.

In 1846, Clay returned to his home and private law practice. During the Civil War, Union troops invaded northern Alabama and Clay was arrested, his home and property seized. However, he survived and lived on quietly in Huntsville until his death in 1866.

Gabriel Moore
1829–March, 1831

John Gayle
1831–1835

Clement Comer Clay
1835–July, 1837

Hugh McVay
July, 1837–November, 1837

HUGH McVAY
(July, 1837–November, 1837)
Lauderdale County

Hugh McVay was one of several Alabama governors who came into that position via the office of president of the state senate. When Governor Clay resigned the governorship in July, 1837, to accept a seat in the U.S. Senate, McVay advanced automatically to the governorship. He served only those intervening months between Clay's departure and the inauguration of Governor Bagby.

McVay was born in South Carolina in 1788, the son of a Revolutionary soldier. He moved to Alabama in 1807, settling as a planter in Madison County. McVay represented that county in the Mississippi territorial legislature from 1811 to 1818. He moved to Lauderdale County in 1819 and was its representative to the Alabama Constitutional Convention of 1819.

McVay served in the lower house of the state legislature from 1820 until 1825 and in the state senate from 1825 until 1837. He was elected president of the senate in 1836.

McVay seems to have been a man of common sense and high integrity, though of mediocre educational background. He was a member of the Methodist Episcopal Church and was married to a Miss Hawks of South Carolina. He died at his home in Lauderdale County in 1851.

ARTHUR PENDLETON BAGBY
(1837–1841)
Monroe County

Arthur Pendleton Bagby, another Virginian, left his home state as a young man and, traveling on foot, arrived in Claiborne, Alabama, Monroe County in the year 1818. Clement Comer Clay, when he migrated to the new country, at least had two horses and a Negro man-servant; Bagby carried everything he owned in a pack on his back. Claiborne was a thriving town on the Alabama River in the new territory, soon to become a state, and Bagby settled there, read law, and was admitted to the bar in 1819. Thus began one of the most remarkable careers of any Alabamian of the nineteenth century.

Bagby came from a distinguished Virginia family, descendants of James Bagby who had settled in Jamestown in 1628. He was born in Louisa County, Virginia in 1794, son of Captain James Bagby and Mary Jones Bagby of Gloucester County. He was unusually well educated and left Virginia, as many others did, because of the depressing financial conditions of the times.

Bagby was tall, handsome, intelligent, of courtly manner, and possessed of a remarkable facility with the English language. His oratory was fiery and colorful, and he immediately attracted the public's attention. At age twenty-one he began his political life with his election to the lower house of the state legislature. In 1822 he was reelected and chosen speaker of the house, the youngest man to hold that office in Alabama in the nineteenth century.

Bagby served in one house or the other until 1836 when he was again elected speaker. In 1837, he ran for governor and was elected by a vote of 21,800 to 17,663 over S. W. Oliver of Conecuh County. He was easily reelected in 1839 over A. F. Hopkins of Madison.

In 1841, Bagby was elected to the U.S. Senate to fill an unexpired term and was again elected, without opposition, to the full six-year term in 1842. He resigned from the Senate in 1848 to accept an appointment by President Polk as minister to the Court of St. Petersburg.

Recalled to the United States after a change of administration in Washington, Bagby was appointed to a commission to codify the statutes of the state of Alabama. This was his last public service. Afterward, he lived in Camden, Wilcox County for several years, then moved to Mobile in 1856 where he died of yellow fever in the autumn of 1858.

Bagby was twice married—first to Emily Steel of Monroe County, earlier of Georgia, and second, in 1828, to Anne Elizabeth Connell of South Carolina. Apparently, his public life was somewhat hampered by his inability to stay out of debt. But there can be little doubt that his service was distinguished.

As governor, Bagby inherited the problem of the state bank, which had been brought into rather lurid perspective during the panic of 1837. He joined with bank president W. D. Stone in an attempt to prohibit the sale of additional bonds and in restricting issuance of paper money. However, the legislature refused to adopt these measures. In his first message to the legislature, Bagby singled out the banking problem as one of "gravest importance," and advised extreme caution in its management. The banks temporarily flourished during his administration, but the system was riding on a bubble; and none of his efforts brought about more than a minimum of reform.

In other areas, Bagby led in the creation of a state penitentiary system, supported the Bestor movement for improved public schools, established the chancery courts, and worked long and tirelessly on improved river navigation.

Another matter, more national in nature, which reared its warning head during Bagby's tenure was the abolitionist movement, coupled with the testy question of states' rights vs federal authority.

Bagby was an ardent states' righter and fiercely pro-slavery. In his message to the legislature on November 2, 1840, he made ringing defense of slavery. At this time, he had begun to doubt, apparently, if the South could continue in the Union along with the abolitionists and their anti-slavery activity, their petitions and propaganda. Bagby admonished, "It is perfectly idle for us, no matter what may be the depth of and sincerity of our attachment to that instrument, to be clinging to the forms of the Constitution while its substance is daily yielding to the rude tide of innovation and fanaticism which is constantly lashing against us."

Bagby had, in 1831, changed his political party from national Republican to Democrat, following his opposition to the national bank and his support of President Jackson on nullification. From then on, he was a Jackson Democrat, and, as such, he supported Van Buren in the election of 1840 against General Harrison, a Whig. In this campaign, Bagby was criticized for being "crude and vulgar." Nevertheless, the Democrats carried the state for Van Buren with a majority of 5,520 votes. In fact, they carried all counties north of the Black Belt and three in the south. With such a mandate, the Democrats then made the mistake of attempting to gerrymander the voting districts by county so that in actuality about five counties in northern Alabama would elect all congressmen. The matter was referred to the legislature and voted down, in spite of the governor's support.

In the early 1850s, Bagby attended the Southern Rights Convention in Nashville, where he opposed the Unionists at every step. The Unionists were advocating that even peaceable secession was unconstitutional. The Southern Rights Convention rejected Henry Clay's Compromise of 1850 regarding slavery in the territories, which was passed by Congress. According to historian A.

B. Moore, "Yancey, Bagby, Seibels, John A. Elmore, George Goldthwaite, and Thomas Williams dominated the convention, which was composed largely of Democrats from the Black Belt. The union convention was made up mainly of Whigs from the same section."

State newspapers were split on the issue. The Pickens *Republican* editorialized, "And let it not be published in Garth nor in the streets of Askelan that we of the South first struck the fatal blow to dissolve this great and glorious monument of our fathers."

Thus, more than a decade before the North and South finally split into two warring nations, a decisive cleft between the leaders of the two major parties in the Deep South state of Alabama was evident.

BENJAMIN FITZPATRICK
(1841–1845)
Autauga (Elmore) County

Benjamin Fitzpatrick, Alabama's eleventh governor, was born in Greene County, Georgia on June 30, 1802, son of William and Anne Phillips Fitzpatrick. His father was a native Virginian who had served as a lieutenant in the Revolutionary War and emigrated to Georgia in 1784.

Benjamin was orphaned at the age of seven; he was then reared by an older sister and brothers. He came to Alabama in 1816 to help manage the plantation of his brothers on the banks of the Alabama River a few miles north of Montgomery. His education was limited, but he made up for this, apparently, very early. After reading law in the office of Nimrod E. Beson of Montgomery, he was admitted to the bar before he was twenty. He was elected solicitor of Montgomery circuit at age seventeen, and was reelected in 1822. He set up a law practice in Montgomery with Henry Goldthwaite and practiced there until 1827 when his health forced his retirement to his plantation, where he remained for the next twelve years.

In his first case as a young lawyer, he was defense attorney for an Indian accused of horse stealing. He won an acquittal but had to take his client out the back door and aid in his flight from the wrath of white citizens.

When Governor Clay resigned his office to go to the U.S. Senate in July of 1837, Fitzpatrick's name was proposed, along with Bagby's, as candidate to fill the vacancy. Bagby won, but Fitzpatrick was now out of retirement and back in politics. In 1839, he headed the Democratic presidential electors, supporting Van Buren. In 1841, he ran against James W. McLung of Madison County for governor and won by a vote of 27,974 to 21,219. He was reelected in 1843 without opposition.

In the 1841 race, Fitzpatrick ran on the bank issue, strongly opposing the state banks (there were then four branches, including the branch at the capital in Tuscaloosa) and their political managers. William L. Yancey and his paper, the Wetumpka *Argus,* supported Fitzpatrick in the contest, which saw bank reformers Yancey, John A. Campbell, and John Erwin elected to the legislature. Campbell was appointed by Fitzpatrick to head the commission on banking.

Again, banking reform was blocked by a coalition of Whigs and Democrats, who were beneficiaries of the bank. However, the legislature began liquidation of the bank in 1842, with arrangements for payment of the bank's debts by the state. In 1845, the bank's charter was not renewed. However, the final Fitzpatrick legislature voted a resolution of confidence in the bank and refused to accept liquidation as final.

In 1845, the Democrats nominated Nathaniel Terry, president of the state senate and a friend of the bank (he owed it $46,049), as candidate to succeed Governor Fitzpatrick. The bank reformers in the party bolted and nominated Joshua L. Martin of Limestone County to run against Terry as an independent. Martin won by 5,000 votes. With this election, the fate of the state bank was decided, but settlement of its affairs took some time. In the end, the legislature did vote a resolution commending Governor Fitzpatrick for his actions in the complicated and grievous banking matter.

The legislature of 1843–1844, following the defeat of the earlier gerrymander effort, attempted to redistrict the state on a basis of the 1840 census. Fitzpatrick recommended apportioning representation on the basis of white population as opposed to "plural voting" or total count, including slaves. This latter, of course, was the choice of large slaveholders. William L. Yancey supported Fitzpatrick's recommendation, and it won over the violent opposition of prominent Whigs.

Coffee County was created during Fitzpatrick's administration, and the towns of Troy and Tuskegee were incorporated.

When U.S. Senator Dixon H. Lewis of Lowndes County died in 1848, Governor Chapman appointed Fitzpatrick to the Senate vacancy. He was again appointed by Governor Collier in 1853 to fill the seat of Rufus King, who had been elected to the vice-presidency. In 1855, Fitzpatrick was elected by the Alabama senate to a full term as U.S. Senator and served until 1861. In December, 1857, he was chosen president pro tempore of the Senate, in the absence of a vice-president, and served in that position until June 12, 1860, the only Alabamian aside from Senator King to ever hold this high office.

Fitzpatrick was nominated at the 1860 Democratic convention in Baltimore for the vice-presidency on the ticket with Judge Stephen A. Douglas, but declined, realizing the hopelessness of the Democratic party's chances, and also because of differences which he had with Douglas on "squatter sovereignty."

When Alabama seceded in 1861, Fitzpatrick left the Senate and returned to Alabama. As a senator he had opposed secession, as had Judge John A. Campbell of Mobile, justice on the U.S. Supreme Court. Both men felt they could go along with a Republican administration, provided it committed no overt act against the South. Following secession, however, Fitzpatrick and Campbell were totally loyal to the Confederacy.

In 1865, along with Governor Watts, ex-Governors Shorter and Moore, and ex-Senator Clay, Fitzpatrick was arrested as a traitor and placed in a northern prison. Released later that year, he represented Autauga County in the Alabama Constitutional Convention of 1865 and was unanimously elected its president. This convention abolished slavery as an institution within the state, declared secession null and void, and provided for the election of officers to state and national offices. However, the U.S. Congress refused to seat the Alabama electees to the House and Senate, and with the passage of the Reconstruction Act of 1867 the period of military rule began in the South.

Fitzpatrick's work in the convention of 1865 was his last public service; he was soon thereafter disenfranchised, along with thousands of other southern leaders.

Fitzpatrick was first married on July 19, 1827, at Huntingdon plantation, Autauga County (in what is now Elmore County) to Sarah Terry Elmore, who died ten years later. He was married again in November, 1846, to Aurelia Rachel Blassingame of Marion.

Fitzpatrick was not only the most handsome public figure of his time, he was also a leader of great stature.

JOSHUA LANIER MARTIN
(1845-1847)
Tuscaloosa County

Joshua Lanier Martin was the gubernatorial candidate chosen by the Democrats who bolted the party in protest over the pro state bank platform at the convention of 1845. They could not have chosen a more able and worthy candidate to carry the battle against the powers of the state bank in Alabama. Martin's record had been consistently anti-bank, and he was a fearless campaigner who felt he was destined to carry out the mandate of the people. It was a bitter campaign. However, Martin, against vicious accusations by the opposition, succeeded in exposing regular Democratic candidate Nathaniel Terry's bank record. Terry was found to be in debt to the state bank in excess of $46,000. Martin was elected by more than a 5,000 vote majority.

Joshua L. Martin was born December 5, 1799, in Blount County, Tennessee, son of Warner and Martha Bailey Martin. He studied law under Reverend Issac Anderson in Maryville, Tennessee and under Reverend Gideon Blackburn. Martin moved to Alabama in 1819 and completed his law studies with his brother in Russellville. He was admitted to the bar shortly thereafter and began his law practice in Athens, Limestone County. He was soon elected the Limestone representative to the state legislature, where he served until 1828 (excepting one year).

Martin was elected solicitor of the fourth judicial circuit in 1829, a position he held until 1834. In that year, he defeated Judge John White of Talladega, an early Alabama supreme court justice, for judge of the circuit court. In 1835, Martin was elected to the U.S. Congress; he was reelected in 1837 and served until 1839. In 1841, he was elected chancellor of the middle chancery division of the state.

Soon after assuming the duties of the governorship, Martin prevailed on the legislature to authorize a commission to make a complete report on the state bank's affairs. The charter of the bank had expired during the Fitzpatrick administration in 1845. However, the banking interests had no idea of giving up. Martin's job was an unpleasant and sometimes dangerous one, but a job he carried out.

Francis S. Lyon of Marengo County was a member of the legislative commission to whom fell the task of winding up the bank's affairs—collection of claims, disposal of physical property, etc. Lyon's performance was superior, but the final work of liquidating the state bank went on until 1858, when all its notes were at last withdrawn from circulation.

The old-line Democrats of Alabama never forgave Martin for the bank's dissolution, and a permanent split in the party seemed inevitable. However, Martin had the generosity and graciousness to withdraw from the campaign to succeed himself in order to prevent a Whig victory. As a result, Reuben Chapman of Madison County was nominated by the Democrats and defeated the Whig candidate, Nicholas Davis.

During Martin's term, the United States declared war on Mexico, and the consequent responsibilities of a wartime governor fell his lot. Toward the end of his administration, in 1847, the capital was moved from Tuscaloosa to the more central location at Montgomery.

Following his term as governor, Martin resumed law practice; he rendered one last public service as representative of his county in the state legislature of 1853.

Martin was twice married—first to Mary Gillam Mason and then to Sarah Ann Mason, both natives of Virginia and sisters to the Honorable William Mason of Limestone County.

Ex-Governor Martin died in Tuscaloosa on November 2, 1856. He had never lost a political race.

REUBEN CHAPMAN
(1847–1849)
Madison County

In 1847, Reuben Chapman left his seat in the U.S. Congress to accept his party's nomination for governor; he did not solicit this nomination—only accepted it. As noted, Joshua Martin had withdrawn from the race to forestall a permanent split in the state Democratic party, and Chapman was the compromise candidate to run against the Whigs. He won over Nicholas Davis, Sr. of Limestone County by a vote of 29,722 to 23,467.

The banking matter had finally been solved, and Governor Chapman set about establishing business-like, economical methods in the state government which would offset, to some extent, the financial damage that had been done by the state bank. In this, he succeeded.

The core problem which Chapman inherited was a more serious and a tragic one—slavery, the agitation against it in the U.S. Congress and throughout the North and the resulting question of the constitutional rights of the slave-holding states. Chapman was a force for restraint and moderation, but the fated course had been charted and no power could turn it back.

Reuben Chapman was born in Caroline County, Virginia in 1802, son of Colonel Reuben Chapman, a colonial soldier, and Ann Reynolds Chapman from Essex County. He moved to Huntsville, Alabama in 1824 and read law in the office of his brother, Samuel Chapman. He was admitted to the bar in 1825 and practiced in Huntsville for a year before moving to Morgan County.

Chapman was elected to the state senate in 1832, and in 1835 won a seat in the U.S. Congress. In 1837, he won reelection over ex-Governor Gabriel Moore in a hard fought campaign. He was thereafter reelected for four successive terms, with opposition only once, in 1841. Then in 1847, he was elected to and assumed the governorship of Alabama.

During his term as governor, the Mexican War ended, Choctaw County was created, Montevallo was incorporated in Shelby County by the legislature, the Mobile and Ohio Railroad was chartered, a state geologist was appointed, and exploration of Alabama's vast underground wealth of minerals and ores was begun.

The end of the Mexican War called for appropriations to pay for new territories; but with the appropriations bill came an amendment, known as the Wilmot Proviso, which would prohibit establishing slavery in any of the new territories. It was finally defeated, but not before it had raised tempers and debates and caused further polarization of factions.

Moved by the anti-slavery agitation and conflict, Governor Chapman sought the advice of John C. Calhoun. Then he recommended to the legislature that a convention representing the people of Alabama be called to make its voice heard and that it provide for a southern convention if Congress further excluded slavery from the territories or abolished it in the District of Columbia.

The convention was never called because the state of Mississippi invited Alabama, along with all other southern states, to meet in Nashville, Tennessee in June, 1850. Chapman also attended a second session of this Southern Rights Convention in November, 1850; but he was one of only five Alabama delegates. This session adjourned after some resolutions repudiating the Clay Compromise. However, the national Democratic party accepted the compromise and simultaneously nominated William Rufus King to the vice-presidency, a seat he won; the next year, another Alabamian, John A. Campbell, was named to the U.S. Supreme Court.

Nevertheless, the invisible lines were drawn in 1850, and more and more people found they could not walk back across them without dishonor. It is interesting to note that it was Governor Chapman who worded the inscription on the Alabama stone in the Washington Monument: "A Union of Equality Adjusted by the Constitution." The irony was most probably not intended by Chapman, but the telling of a prophecy.

Reuben Chapman retired to his home overlooking the town of Huntsville in 1850. He was recalled once when his party demanded he run against the American party candidate, Colonel Jeremiah Clemens, for the legislature in 1855, a race Chapman won.

He attended the Democratic Convention of 1860 in Baltimore as a Conservative and made valiant effort to bring about some reconciliation in the northern and southern wings of the party. But it was a futile last stand of wisdom against emotion.

Chapman's last official office was as elector for Jefferson Davis for president of the Confederacy in 1862. During the war, his home was burned, he was arrested and imprisoned by northern troops, and he lost a son on the battlefield.

Arthur Pendleton Bagby
1837–1841

Benjamin Fitzpatrick
1841–1845

Joshua Lanier Martin
1845–1847

Reuben Chapman
1847–1849

HENRY WATKINS COLLIER
(1849–1853)
Tuscaloosa County

Henry Watkins Collier was yet another native of Virginia who became an Alabama governor. Collier had everything which a well-to-do, aristocratic family of the time could offer. Born January 17, 1801, in Lunenburg County, Virginia, son of James and Elizabeth Roudin Collier, he was moved at age one with his family to Abbeville District, South Carolina. In 1818, he moved to the newly opened cottonlands in Madison County, Alabama Territory.

Collier was educated in the well-known school of Dr. Moses Waddel of South Carolina. He studied law in Nashville under Judge John Haywood of the Tennessee supreme court and was admitted to the Alabama bar in 1822. The following year, he moved to Tuscaloosa, Alabama and set up a law practice. In 1826, he married Mary Ann Battle of North Carolina, sister of a colleague in Tuscaloosa. Collier was a prominent lifelong member of the Methodist Church. The prominence of Methodists and Presbyterians from among the old Virginia aristocracy and among pioneer leaders of Alabama seems amazing in view of the traditional belief that all Virginia's aristocracy belonged to the Church of England.

Collier was elected to the Alabama legislature in 1827; in 1828 he was elected by that body to the state supreme court, where he served until 1830. In 1836, Governor Clay reappointed him to the supreme court to fill a vacancy, and the legislature confirmed this by electing him formally to that seat. The following year, Collier was elected chief justice, a distinguished office in which he served twelve consecutive years. Apparently, Collier was a careful, scholarly, and detailed jurist. His work was painstaking and thorough.

He was everything non-political, a man of quiet dignity, scholarly demeanor, and certainly not a likely candidate for governor in this perilous decade. But in 1849 the Democratic party selected Collier in convention as a compromise candidate over John Erwin, John A. Winston, and Judge G. W. Stone. He won by a startling 36,350 votes to 364 for his nearest opponent. The conservative element of the party was strong, and it was behind him solidly.

In the election of 1851, Collier refused to take the stump, preferring to run on his dignified record. The big issue was the Compromise of 1850. William L. Yancey represented the pro-southern faction of the Democratic party, and B. G. Shields the pro-Union faction. Collier, always the moderate, stood somewhere between them. Yancey refused to run, and the southern rights faction accepted Collier as a compromise candidate. In this second term race, he won over B. G. Shields, Union Democrat from Marengo County, by an overwhelming 37,460 votes to 5,747.

In his first inaugural address on December 17, 1849, Collier made his views on the slavery and states' rights matters clear. He stated that should a convention of slave states be held, "Alabama will be there. . . . She will present an unbroken front to insult and usurpation."

When the heated debates reached a crescendo in Congress, sparked by the Wilmot Proviso—which never passed the Congress but which led eventually to the Compromise Act of 1850, Governor Collier called on the legislature to convene and select delegates to the Nashville Convention in June. They did so, electing eight delegates at large and four from each congressional district.

After Congress passed the Compromise Act in September, the reaction in the South was mixed. Many in Alabama urged the governor to ask the legislature to provide for a state convention on southern rights. However, Collier, cautious and conservative, preferred to wait until after the November session of the convention in Nashville. This session accomplished little, but the Compromise Act had caused deep divisions in southern party ranks. Collier, ever the conciliator and mediator, did an unbelievable job of restoring some unanimity and order to the Alabama Democratic party.

However, the extreme Unionists and secessionists held out. The secessionists reorganized the Southern Rights party, which made it known they were against this compromise or any other and had no idea of conforming. They met in national convention and nominated candidates for president and vice-president.

The Whigs were finally drawn toward the major southern sentiment of strong states' rights, but in their national convention committed the party to the Compromise. At the same time, the southern faction warned their northern brothers, according to A. B. Moore, that "if anti-slavery agitation was to continue they would stand by their people and their property under the banner of Southern Rights."

By this time, it must have been clear to all that the South would never stand by and see its constitutional rights trampled. But the North blundered on and, carrying with it the heavy moral cudgel of anti-slavery, finally drove the southern states from the Union. Perhaps it was necessary, but one wonders if moderation on both sides had prevailed a few years longer, would not the slaves have been eventually freed by the individual states, and without the nightmare which began in 1861 and lasted for over a hundred years—subsiding only late in the twentieth century.

Collier was among the southern leaders who helped to free the South of dependence on the North by encouraging development of southern industry, particularly of textile manufacturing, since the mills would be so close to the raw product. The textile industry which had grown rapidly in the decade of the forties (there were twelve textile mills in Alabama in 1850), continued to expand throughout the decade of the fifties.

The governor followed the philosophy of Judge Benjamin F. Porter of Tuscaloosa in overhauling the school system. He believed in an equal division of funds among townships and centralized control over the whole system.

Collier was also deeply interested in the humanitarian efforts of Dorothea Dix and helped her in gaining some measure of prison reform in Alabama.

On his retirement from the governorship, Collier was offered a seat in the U.S. Senate, but ill health prevented his accepting. He died only two years later at Bailey Springs, Alabama, in the year 1855.

JOHN ANTHONY WINSTON
(1853–1857)
Sumter County

John A. Winston was the first native-born Alabamian to become governor of the state. But he too was of Virginia descent. His grandfather Anthony Winston, an officer in the Revolutionary army, was born in Hanover County, Virginia, but moved to Madison County in the Mississippi Territory in 1810. Governor Winston's parents, William and Mary Baker Winston, were living in Madison County when he was born on September 4, 1812.

Winston's early education was in private schools, and he later attended Cumberland College in Tennessee (later the University of Nashville). Contrary to the tradition of Alabama governors, Winston did not become a lawyer. Outside of politics, he had two main occupations —planter and cotton commissioner. Winston purchased his first plantation in 1834 in Sumter County and remained at the task of its management, with great success, for some ten years, at which time he opened a cotton commission house in Mobile. The cotton commissioner of this period was a key figure in the mercantile procedure, an important and trusted agent. Winston was twice married, first in 1832 to Mary Agnes Walker who died in 1842, and then to Mary W. Logwood. Apparently, this second marriage ended in divorce in 1850.

Winston was elected to the Alabama house of representatives in 1840 and again in 1842. In 1843, he was elected to the state senate where he remained for ten years, until 1853, serving as senate president from 1845 to 1849. Because of his strong-willed temperament and because of his personal animosity toward William L. Yancey, controversy swirled about Winston almost constantly.

At the Democratic convention called in Montgomery on February 14, 1848, the slave-holding interests faced strong opposition from the "Hunkers" or mountaineers from the non-slave-holding counties of northern Alabama. William L. Yancey, through the sheer force of his oratory, swept all opposition before him; and his resolutions, which were passed by nearly unanimous vote, became known as the "Alabama Platform." This convention instructed its delegates to the subsequent general convention in Baltimore to oppose any candidate for president who did not "speak out against the Wilmot Proviso," or even "squatter sovereignty" (actually popular sovereignty, which was simply the provision that the people of a new territory were to determine if it would be slave or free).

However, there was trepidation at home that Yancey had gone too far, that the Whigs would benefit from such extremes. At the Baltimore convention, John A. Winston, delegate-at-large, led a revolt of Alabama delegates against Yancey and his platform, throwing their support to Cass, who was known as a supporter of squatter sovereignty. This was in defiance of the instructions to the delegates, and their action rent the Democratic party in Alabama. Cass carried the state by 881 votes.

In the legislature of 1849 called by Governor Chapman, which broadcast resolutions opposing popular sovereignty and all other anti-slavery measures, Winston entered a final resolution hinting that if Congress defied any of the Alabama resolutions, the state's delegates would resign. Some inconsistency is obvious here, to say the least.

In 1850, Winston was one of the eight delegates-at-large from Alabama chosen to attend the Nashville convention. By the time he ran for governor in 1853, he was known as a strong southern rights man.

In 1853, he was nominated by the Democrats to run against Whig candidate Richard W. Walker; however, Walker retired from the race due to ill health, and Winston won easily against scattered opposition.

Governor Winston was opposed to using state monies in support of public transportation facilities, mainly the railroads. He was opposed to it on principle and because of the state indebtedness following failure of the state bank. However, the forces in favor of state aid were strong, bringing the governor and his legislature into acid conflict, in the course of which Winston vetoed some thirty bills passed by the legislature and became known as the "veto governor." The legislature, who disliked his stiffness and sarcasm, began to take the Winston veto as a matter of course and passed many bills over it. But undoubtedly, Governor Winston saved thousands of dollars in tax money which otherwise would have gone to support private business interests.

But along with such admirable stance, Winston managed, incongruously, to veto a bill appropriating $150,000 for completion of a state hospital for the insane. He was totally committed to aid to education and in 1854 signed the bill which created a statewide public school system, sponsored by A. B. Meek and Willoughby Barton of Mobile and modeled on the Mobile school system.

In the gubernatorial race of 1855, the Know Nothing party entered Alabama politics on a platform of reform, which apparently meant reforming everyone who disagreed with them or anyone who was Catholic or of foreign birth. And they received considerable support; there were even some floggings of Catholics and "foreigners" in the old civilized city of Mobile.

The Know Nothing candidate was Judge George D. Shortridge of Montgomery, and the debate which followed between him and Winston was bitter and filled with denunciation. Winston was superb on the debate stand, with a quick wit, strong irony, and vivid imagery. The campaign grew so bitter that Winston at one point challenged a man to a duel who had accused him of being a Know Nothing. Subsequently, Thomas H. Watts, candidate for Congress, challenged Winston. Winston declined this one on the grounds that Watts "was not a gentleman."

The 1855 voting was the heaviest in the history of the state to that time. Winston won by a vote of 42,238 to 30,636 for Shortridge. At the conclusion of his second term, Winston recommended to his legislature that Alabama begin military preparedness as a result of the border war in "Bleeding Kansas," violence brought on by the same old conflict—free soilers vs slave-holders.

During the Civil War, Winston was made colonel of the Eighth Alabama Regiment. A too strict disciplinarian and unpopular with his men, he nevertheless served with distinction in the Peninsular Campaign. Following a year's service in combat, ill health forced him to resign the army and return to his plantation.

Winston was elected a delegate to the Alabama Constitutional Convention of 1865. In 1867, he was elected to the U.S. Senate but was refused his seat by Congress. Shortly thereafter, he, along with thousands of other former Confederate leaders, was disenfranchised.

He died in Mobile on December 21, 1871.

ANDREW BARRY MOORE
(1857–1861)
Perry County

To Governor Andrew Barry Moore fell the grave responsibility of presiding over Alabama's secession from the Union and the beginning days of the long dreaded Civil War. Following the election of Lincoln, reaction in Alabama and elsewhere throughout the South was immediate and violent in intensity. Southern rights leaders now witnessed both the executive and legislative branches of the federal government fall into the hands of the "Black Republicans"; to them, it meant the end—no more compromise or procrastination.

Governor Moore took immediate steps to have the people of the state voice their intentions at the polls.

Christmas Eve, 1860, was the appointed day for the voters to elect their delegates to a secession convention.

These delegates, duly elected, met at Montgomery on January 7, 1861, in what later became the chamber of the house of representatives. These secessionist delegates were of two stamps—"straight-outs" who wanted immediate secession of the state and "cooperationists" who wanted to wait and act in concert with other southern states. The straight-outs were representatives largely of southern and central Alabama, although the Whigs of the Black Belt generally supported cooperation; the cooperationists were representatives of northern Alabama. The evidence of this deep division was clear when, in spite of William L. Yancey's fiery oratory, the delegates voted to secede by a margin of only 61 to 39. South Carolina had already seceded on December 20, 1860.

The convention authorized Governor Moore to raise 500 troops and appropriated $10 thousand for aid to Governor Percy of Florida in seizing the federal forts at Pensacola. As a final key action, the delegates voted to issue an invitation to all slave-holding states to meet in convention at Montgomery on February 4, 1861.

This convention was to become the Provisional Congress of the Confederacy, and, as such, it organized a provisional government. On February 9, the congress elected a president and vice-president. Two weeks later, on February 18, Jefferson Davis took the oath of office on the capitol portico as president of the Confederate States of America.

In the meantime, between the election of the delegates to the state convention and the meeting of that convention on January 7, Governor Moore had ordered, on January 4, the seizure of Fort Morgan, Fort Gaines, and the federal arsenal at Mt. Vernon. Moore was criticized for this action, but it proved to be a far-sighted strategic military move. If Moore had been able to remain governor or to hold a powerful position in the Confederate government, the South's fortunes might have fared better. He put aside states' rights and petty interests and threw every effort into the great trials facing the Confederacy. Some who followed him failed to do this. This senseless, petty division of interests was the South's worst enemy, existing inside itself.

Following secession, the Alabama legislature met in special session and appropriated $509 thousand, authorizing issuance of treasury notes and sale of 8 percent bonds for the defense effort.

Alabamians began enlisting faster than they could be provided for. By October, 1861, Governor Moore reported Alabama had 27,000 soldiers and officers in the field.

Andrew Barry Moore, sixteenth governor of Alabama, was born March 7, 1807, in Spartanburg District, North Carolina, the son of Captain Charles and Jane Barry Moore. Captain Moore had been a soldier in the Revolutionary War and in the War of 1812.

In 1826, young Moore came to Perry County, Alabama. Because of his excellent early education, he was prevailed upon to settle there and teach school. He taught for two years and in the meantime read law in the office of Elisha Young and Sidney Goode. He was admitted to the bar in 1833. In 1837 he married Mary Gorce of Perry County. He was a Presbyterian.

Moore was elected to the legislature in 1839, re-elected in 1842, and served four consecutive terms. Three times he served as speaker of the house. Moore was chosen elector for Cass in the presidential election of 1848. In 1851, he was appointed judge on the circuit court, was elected to that position the next year, and served until he resigned in 1857 to accept the Democratic party's nomination for governor. He was elected without opposition.

The Whig party was definitely on the decline, but the southern rights wing led by William F. Samford, an able writer in the southern cause, opposed Moore in the 1859 election. Samford ran as an "Independent Southern Rights Candidate." His argument was that Governor Moore had done too little to espouse the cause of southern rights. However, Moore had taken some steps. Following John Brown's raid on Harper's Ferry, July 3, 1859, the Moore legislature had appropriated $200 thousand for defense and provided for raising 8,000 volunteers for the militia. Military training was begun for students at the University of Alabama. Moore was victorious over Samford by a decisive majority.

During Moore's two terms, the Alabama Hospital for the Insane was established at Tuscaloosa, with Dr. Peter Bryce its first superintendent. The Medical College, a branch of the University of Alabama, was established in Mobile, and the Institute for the Deaf was established at Talladega. Education improved during this period, until the outbreak of the war. The census of 1860 showed Alabama's population stood at 964,201.

At the end of his term as governor, Moore was appointed special aide-de-camp to Governor Shorter. Following the surrender, ex-Governor Moore was seized and imprisoned at Ft. Pulaski, Savannah, along with ex-Governors Shorter, Clay, and Fitzpatrick.

He was released later that same year because of failing health. He returned to Marion in his old home county to practice law and died there on April 5, 1873.

JOHN GILL SHORTER
(1861–1863)
Barbour County

John Gill Shorter's administration witnessed a magnificent surge of patriotic war effort. Shortly thereafter, however, as the burdens of war increased, Union troops invaded northern Alabama, and President Davis lost popularity, this southern patriotism degenerated into a niggling, short-sighted reluctance to support the Confederacy, and in some matters after 1863 became obstructionist.

Shorter was elected governor in 1861 while he was a member of the Provisional Congress in Richmond. Opposing him was Thomas E. Watts of Montgomery; the vote was 37,849 to 28,127. Two years later, Watts defeated Shorter by a vote of nearly four to one; at the same time, six pacifist candidates, enemies of Davis, were elected to the Confederate Congress.

In the beginning, the people were behind Governor Shorter and his untiring efforts to construct defenses (especially at the vital port of Mobile), to raise troops, to care for the families of soldiers, and to support without stint the Confederacy in its life and death struggle. But taxes grew heavy, conscription increased, and too many of the loyal men were away at war. Inspired by efforts of the peace party and becoming more distrustful of Davis, the voters did an about-face in 1863 and repudiated the principles of that governor whose vision and courage went beyond the purely personal and local interests to that single, vital, and overpowering necessity—defeat of the enemy.

Some former leaders of the old anti-secessionist group—including William H. Smith (later appointed Alabama governor by act of Congress in July, 1868), Jeremiah Clemens, cousin of Mark Twain, and George Lane —went over to the federals. Others, still loyal to the South but believing an early peace the best solution, wanted the war party out and stumped the state against Shorter; among them was L. E. Parsons, later appointed interregnum governor in June, 1865.

In August, 1863, a little over a month after Gettysburg, the people of Alabama—those who remained at
home, those who cast votes to defeat Shorter—gave tacit
assent to the growing poison of defeatism. Ex-Governor
Shorter retired to his law practice in Eufala; it was the
end of his political life and his dynamic leadership in the
southern cause.

John Gill Shorter was born in Monticello, Georgia on
April 23, 1818, the son of General Reuben C. Shorter
and Martha Gill Shorter. General Shorter, a native of
Virginia, had moved to Georgia as a young man.

John graduated from Franklin College in Athens,
Georgia (later the University of Georgia) in 1837 and
came to Barbour County, Alabama where he studied law
and was admitted to the bar in 1838. He was married to
Mary Jane Battle of Eufala on January 12, 1843.

In 1842, Shorter was appointed solicitor of his district; and in 1845 he was elected to the state senate. He
served in the senate two years and then returned to his
law practice. But the challenge of the times was too great
for a man of his discernment and loyalties. He entered
public life again in 1851 and was elected to the lower
house of the legislature. That same year, Shorter was
appointed judge on the circuit court. He ran for this
same judgeship the next year, was elected to serve six
years, and was reelected in 1858. When Governor Moore
appointed him as representative from Alabama to the
secession convention in the state of Georgia, he resigned
the bench and, from that time on, was embroiled in the
great crisis of the nation.

Shorter was strong in his Confederate loyalty, helped
to frame the Confederate constitution, and later was representative in the Provisional Confederate Congress,
where he supported Davis in all his recommendations
and never failed to vote in support of Davis' vetoes. From

Henry Watkins Collier
1849–1853

John Anthony Winston
1853–1857

Andrew Barry Moore
1857–1861

John Gill Shorter
1861–1863

this position, Shorter resigned to return home and assume office as wartime governor of his state.

W. Brewer writes of him: "Governor Shorter was of ordinary height, with a delicate figure, and an intellectual cast of features. He was without arrogance or ostentation and had the most unaffected mildness and simplicity of manners. He served the State ably and faithfully; appearing to have no other purpose in office but to 'execute justice and maintain truth.' "

John Gill Shorter died in Eufala on May 29, 1872.

THOMAS HILL WATTS
(1863–April, 1865)
Montgomery County

Thomas Hill Watts was the third Alabama governor to hold that office during the trials of the Civil War. Moore's term had been for a relatively short period; Shorter's was during the early phase, one of high war spirit; Watts' was undoubtedly the most tragic period of all. From the governor's chair, Watts saw the walls come tumbling down. Perhaps it was, in part, some of his own fault.

Watts was a loyal southerner, no doubt of that, even though he had been a Whig and strongly anti-secessionist before the election of Lincoln. After that election, however, he felt that there was no hope in any course but separation from the Union. He moved into the secessionist camp with all his great force and talents, was a leader in the secession convention, and first ran for governor in 1861. The *Southern Messenger* of November 21, 1860 quotes Watts: "A piratical, fanatical crew has taken possession, and now stands erect, in haughty defiance, on the deck of the old Ship Constitution. . . . The vilest oppressions and the grandest frauds and tyrannies the world ever saw have been perpetrated under the forms of law and Constitution."

Watts raised, and served as colonel, over his own regiment, the Seventeenth Alabama. On April 9, 1862, he accepted President Davis' appointment to become attorney general of the Confederacy, an office he resigned when he was elected governor in 1863.

The fervor of his oratory in his inaugural address indicated the tone of his feelings: "From the Gulf to our northern border; from the mountains, valleys and plains; from the east and from the west, the stalwart sons of Alabama rushed to the standard of the newborn republic; and with dauntless bravery and heroism they have crimsoned with their blood every battlefield from Manassas to Chickamauga."

In his first message to the legislature, Watts declared, "He who is now . . . in favor of reconstruction with the States under Lincoln's dominion is a traitor in his heart to the State . . . and deserves a traitor's doom." These are strong words and, for the time, perhaps moving oratory. But Watts with all his zeal failed to create, organize, and provide the Confederacy the unified support of the state which, along with similar support from every state in the Confederacy, might have made the difference between defeat and victory.

Northern Alabama was being invaded as early as 1863; the Confederacy lost the Battle of Mobile Bay and Fort Morgan in August, 1864; Wilson's invading army burned the University of Alabama, then the arsenal at Selma (along with the town) in 1865. In northern Alabama, there was savage destruction, along with murder, rape and pillage in such towns as Athens, Huntsville, Florence, and Decatur—all in the best tradition of Attila the Hun. The people were suffering, and Governor

Watts made every effort to alleviate that suffering. Somewhere along the way, his vision of the great goal was lost in the local holocaust. His adamant stand on states' rights in the midst of a desperate military struggle, when every state, every individual, needed to work together, is somewhat mystifying. He opposed Jefferson Davis on the matter of conscription; he threatened the Confederate general in charge of conscription in Alabama with intervention by the state authorities, meaning military force. He opposed Davis on impressment of private property; he refused to allow elected local officials to be drafted into the army, even though they might have been elected after the Conscription Act of February, 1864.

However, there was much worse opposition at large in the state in the form of the traitorous "peace society," whose members at one time were ready to seize the state government in armed rebellion. Watts stood unmoved against their insidious suggestions and threats.

When the Confederacy fell, Watts lost his considerable property, his term as governor was cut short by the conquering power, and he was summarily arrested and imprisoned in the North. He was released shortly thereafter and finally pardoned by President Johnson in 1868.

Thomas Hill Watts was born January 3, 1819, near the modern town of Greenville in what was then Alabama Territory, the son of John Hughes and Frances Watts; he was of Virginia descent. He attended the local schools as a boy, and then his father offered him money, "in lieu of any further claim upon the family estate," to attend the University of Virginia. Watts graduated from that university in 1839. In 1840, he was admitted to the Alabama bar and practiced in Greenville, later establishing a practice in Montgomery.

Very early in his career, Watts joined the Whig party. Throughout his life, he seems to have been involved in politics, serving three terms in the legislature from Butler County and twice from Montgomery County. For a while, he was involved with the Know Nothing party and ran unsuccessfully for Congress on their ticket in 1856.

Like many other Whigs, Watts was strongly anti-secessionist and pro-Union. Only after the election of Lincoln did he change his views and ally himself with Yancey and the states' rights wing of the Democratic party.

Watts was twice married—first, to Eliza Brown Allen, who died in 1847; second, to Ellen Noyes Jackson in 1875. He was a Baptist and very active in the church.

He died in Montgomery on September 16, 1892.

Watts obviously had the qualities for great leadership. His short-sightedness in the conduct of the war as governor spelled the crucial difference between him and Governor Shorter.

LEWIS E. PARSONS
(June, 1865–December, 1865)
Talladega County

Lewis E. Parsons, a native of New York, moved to Alabama in 1840. Appointed provisional governor of Alabama on June 21, 1865, he was the first of six Alabama Reconstruction governors.

Actually, Alabama was somewhat fortunate in the men it elected (or who were appointed) to this office in that period; only two of the six—William H. Smith and David P. Lewis, both of whom had deserted the Confederacy during the war—supported wholeheartedly the oppressive carpetbagger rule, and the vengeful Reconstruction program of the Republican Congress.

From the beginning, Parsons was strongly anti-secessionist and pro-Union. Even though there were rumors that he was a member of the "peace society" during the war, he seems to have been loyal to the South. The overriding concern of Parsons' political life before the war apparently was preservation of the Union. In 1856, he voted for Fillmore, and he supported Douglas in the 1860 campaign, believing that his election was the only course to save the country. During the war, he supported Watts for governor and was instrumental in the overthrow of the state war party in 1863. Even though he supported Governor Watts in his anti-conscription measures, Parsons was able to oppose the establishment of the state militia, believing that the Confederacy should provide full power in the military field.

During the widespread lawlessness of 1865, when roving bands of recently freed Negroes and discharged federal soldiers committed robbery, murder, rape, and arson almost at will, Parsons called on General Wagner Swayne, in command of the Freedman's Bureau, to bring military force to bear in those counties where crime was at its worst. He worked in harmony with the fair and efficient Swayne in an attempt to feed the starving people, white and black, of the state, making one western trip to procure food and supplies. In December, 1865, Parsons estimated that 250,000 people in Alabama were in dire need of food. Actually, with the state government being dictated largely from Washington, both Parsons and Swayne were handicapped in their efforts to bring about sane Reconstruction and a stable government.

As ex-governor, Parsons together with Alexander White led the "White Man's Movement" in the constitutional election of 1868. Their resolutions in favor of government by respectable whites instead of "strangers, deserters, and bushwhackers," made a strong impres-

sion on reasonable people in the North, but their time
had not yet come. The constitution failed of adoption by
13,550 votes. When William Smith was appointed governor by an act of Congress in July, 1868, rule by the
carpetbaggers and the radical, vengeful element of the
Republican Congress began with all its terrifying reality.

Lewis Parsons was born at Lisle, New York on April
28, 1817, son of Erastus Bellamy and Jennett Hepburn
Parsons. He was educated in the public schools of New
York and later read law in New York and Philadelphia.
When he moved to Talladega, Alabama in 1840, Parsons set up a law practice with Alexander White, one of
Alabama's brilliant jurists and orators. In 1859, he was
elected to the legislature on a program for state aid for
internal improvements. In September, 1841, he married
Jane Ann Boyd Chrisman of Kentucky. Parsons represented Talladega County a second time in the legislature
in 1863. He was chosen senator to the U.S. Congress in
December, 1865, but he was refused his seat by the Congress.

During his short term as provisional governor, Parsons ordered elections on August 31, 1865, of delegates
to a state convention which would form a state government. This body assembled in September, 1865, and was
dominated by the old order—secessionists led by John
A. Elmore, with former governor Benjamin Fitzpatrick
elected presiding officer. The convention declared
secession "null and void," repudiated the state debts of
the Confederacy, legally abolished slavery, and provided
for elections in November.

In these elections, Robert Patton was elected governor over William Smith and Bulger, both deserters of the
Confederacy; and Parsons, along with George Huston,
was elected to the Senate. Both senators-elect were refused their seats. Patton's tenure was cut short, for in

July, 1867, General Swayne was appointed military governor. He was succeeded by William H. Smith in the July elections of 1868, and the darkest and most inexplicable hour of Reconstruction was upon Alabama.

In spite of his efforts on behalf of the state, Parsons chose in 1870 to go over to the Radical party, supporting Smith against Lindsay (even advising Smith to contest the election which he had lost). And in the election of 1872, he supported Radical candidate Spencer for the state senate. Spencer controlled federal patronage in Alabama and was elected, giving Governor Lewis a majority Radical legislature.

In 1872–1873 Parsons, remaining in the Radical party, was speaker of the Republican house in the legislature. This ended his political career in Alabama because the great surge forward of the Democratic party and the establishment of white man's rule in Alabama were already making their entries at both wings of the stage.

Parsons continued the practice of law in Alabama until his death on June 8, 1895.

ROBERT M. PATTON
(December, 1865–July, 1867)
Lauderdale County

Robert M. Patton, native Virginian, wealthy planter, early Alabama industrialist and statesman, was the archetype of those southern Whigs who, although opposing secession, when it came acted in complete loyalty and support of their home state and the Confederacy. None gave more than Patton, who lost two sons on the battlefield, saw his large estate laid waste by the enemy, and gave a fortune as well as his considerable talents and energies to support the Confederacy. His work as a commissioner in the Confederate government brought millions of dollars into the treasury of the Confederate war fund.

His work as governor in the post-war period of occupation, with his every action subject to approval of the military authority, was as dedicated, determined, and effective as could have been. He worked in the closest cooperation with General Swayne and was able, during his short tenure, not only to effect some meaningful fiscal policy for the state government and save the devastated South many taxes, but to save more than 30,000 destitute people from starvation.

Patton was born on July 10, 1809, in Russell County, Virginia, son of William and Martha Lee Hays Patton. He moved with his parents to Huntsville in 1818, where his father helped found the Bell cotton mill, the first such plant in Alabama.

Young Robert attended the Green Academy of Huntsville, one of the notable educational institutions in Alabama during the state's formative years. He later was apprenticed in the family business and in 1829 moved to Florence where he took up the mercantile business. Not only did Patton successfully manage this business, he also operated his 3,000-acre plantation, doing both for nearly thirty years. He was married January 31, 1832, to Jane Locke Weakly Brahan of Huntsville. He was a lifelong Presbyterian. He had a large family and his sons took over the mercantile business in the mid-1850s.

Although he was a Whig, Patton was elected to the state legislature from Lauderdale County in 1832 and later, in 1837, to the special legislature called to remedy the severe financial depression of that year. He served several terms in the Alabama legislature between that time and the outbreak of war and was president of the senate when hostilities began.

Patton served at the Charleston convention of 1860 and later at the state convention in Montgomery which took Alabama out of the Union. After the war, he represented Lauderdale County at the Alabama Constitutional Convention of 1865. In the elections which followed in December, he defeated William R. Smith and W. R. Bulger by a vote approximately equal to theirs combined.

In 1867, he issued the famous "Patton certificates" which enabled Alabama to finance its operation prior to the collection of taxes; all these certificates were paid off in federal currency before the end of his term. In addition to operating the state on a sound fiscal basis and feeding thousands of starving people, Patton helped convince Congress to suspend collection of the war tax from the southern states, a potentially ruinous tax on a destitute people.

He first opposed the Fourteenth Amendment but later, convinced by General Swayne that Congress would pass it anyway (which they did), he decided it would be wiser not to resist it. He worked closely with Swayne in an attempt to make the Freedman's Bureau a just and effective means of aiding the southern Negroes and destitute whites, but this effort was destined to ultimate failure.

In March, 1867, the Congress passed the Reconstruction Act which brought an end to the efforts at presidential Reconstruction and ushered in congressional Reconstruction. Patton's was the last legitimate effort of a duly elected Alabama governor to make Reconstruction work and bring the state back into the Union on some honorable and reasonable basis, until the long, nasty series of events came to an end with the inauguration of George Houston in 1874. In July, 1867, Patton

Thomas Hill Watts
1863–April, 1865

Lewis E. Parsons
June, 1865–December, 1865

Robert M. Patton
December, 1865–July, 1867

William H. Smith
July, 1868–November, 1870

was removed officially as governor and replaced by the military governor, General Wagner Swayne.

Patton was later active in establishing and building several southern railroads, among them the South and North Alabama Road and the Mobile and Chattanooga Road. He was on the Board of Trustees for the University of Alabama and was instrumental in the rebuilding of the university, burned in Croxton's raid of 1865.

Patton died February 28, 1885, and was buried at Huntsville.

WAGNER SWAYNE
(July, 1867–July, 1868)
Military Governor

General Swayne was never elected governor of Alabama. While serving as a commissioner of the Freedman's Bureau from 1865 to January, 1869, he was appointed military governor of Alabama in July, 1867, and served until the election of W. H. Smith the following July.

We are accustomed to think of military governors during an occupation as invariably bestial and overbearing; nothing could be further from the fact concerning General Swayne. He was a highly educated gentleman, a distinguished officer of the U.S. Army with a long combat record which included the loss of a leg and the award of the Medal of Honor for bravery in the battle of Corinth on October 4, 1862.

Swayne was graduated from Yale in 1856 and from the Cincinnati Law School in 1859. He practiced law with his father in Columbus, Ohio (his father was later appointed a justice of the U.S. Supreme Court). On August

31, 1861, Swayne entered the army with the rank of major, and this career included in its last phase his service as commander of the Alabama Freedman's Bureau and his one-year tenure as military governor of the state and promotion to major general.

In his service to the country and to the state which he governed under military edict, Swayne proved to be just, fair, compassionate, and reasonable; none of the petty vindictiveness which motivated the actions of the Republican Congress, to which he was, of course, subordinate, rubbed off on his gallant nature. He was given an unpleasant job to do under unpleasant circumstances, and he did it well, in spite of interference from the vengeance-seekers.

During his command in 1865, the Freedman's Bureau forced the state to open courts to the Negroes and give them full civil rights. Court officials and law enforcement officers were sworn into the bureau and came directly under its control. Laws were passed for protection of the Negro. Swayne cooperated with Governors Parsons and Patton, administered the relief measures fairly and efficiently, and was particularly successful in establishing a number of schools.

Swayne attempted to make the bureau work for the effective reconstruction of the whole South. And possibly he would have succeeded, except for the invasion of the carpetbaggers, the opportunistic, propagandizing, partly criminal element which used the Negro and the tragic condition of the defeated South for their personal gain. The Union League, a radical political action group in the Republican party, took the lead and organized the Negro vote with both fake promises and physical force until the carpetbag element was in complete control and all hope of peaceful racial relations went out the window. During the resulting turmoil and agitation, many

Negroes turned lawless, and insurrection was a constant fear, Swayne himself disarmed several bands of blacks.

The Radical party in the convention of November, 1867, dominated by carpetbaggers and scalawags and presided over by Elisha Peck, created a new state constitution. When this constitution came into effect on June 25, 1868, Alabama was readmitted to the Union. On the irony of such paradox does much of history ride.

William H. Smith was elected governor in July, 1868. With the "proud" status of new statehood, Alabama entered into the most humiliating and comi-tragic period of its history.

General Swayne returned to the practice of law, first in Toledo and later in New York, where he died on December 18, 1902.

WILLIAM H. SMITH
(July, 1868–November, 1870)
Randolph County

Historian A. B. Moore describes William H. Smith as "narrow, vindictive, and proved to be unfit for office." There is little which need be added to this laconic summary, except for a few basic facts.

Smith was born in Georgia in 1828 and moved with his parents to Randolph County, Alabama in 1839. He read law and was admitted to the bar in 1850. From 1855 until 1859 he represented Randolph County in the legislature, and in 1860 he was on the Douglas electoral ticket. He was a lifelong Whig and adamantly opposed to secession.

In 1862, Smith deserted to the federals and served in a civilian capacity against the Confederacy until the end of the war. Parsons appointed him judge of the circuit court in 1865, but he resigned it in 1866. Under the congressional Reconstruction Act, he was appointed chief of the Registration Bureau for Alabama.

Smith ran for governor in 1865 and was defeated by Patton, but was elected in July, 1868, by the carpetbag forces. Also elected were A. J. Applegate, carpetbag lieutenant governor, and E. W. Peck, carpetbag chief justice of the Alabama supreme court. Had they flown the jolly roger over the state capitol, there might have been some humorous justice in their inconceivable travesties in the name of government, but they flew the stars and stripes.

Republicans were in complete control of both houses, and the state government was corrupt. Twenty-six seats in the lower house and one in the senate were held by illiterate Negroes; twenty members of the house were either under or had been under indictment for crimes. The delegation to Congress were all carpetbaggers; and the two U.S. senators (seated this time) were Willard Warner, former staff officer to General William T. Sherman, and the notorious wheeler-dealer chief of the carpetbaggers, New Yorker George Spencer.

Alabama's public debt rose to a figure three times the sum it was when Smith entered office. The Fourteenth and Fifteenth Amendments were ratified by the legislature.

Local government was almost as bad, and the election or appointment of ignorant illiterates to high office was commonplace. A former Negro slave, freed in 1865, was made a city judge in Selma. Loyal southern whites of the old Confederacy were helpless, humiliated, and angered. Out of their frustration and bitterness grew the order of the Ku Klux Klan, a last resort to secret vigilantism in order to destroy lawlessness stemming from the very halls of government.

This incumbent parody of a governor ran to succeed himself in 1870 and was narrowly defeated by Lindsay with a vote of 77,721 to 76,292. Smith contested the election, refused to step down, and called in federal troops. By some star-crossed miracle, the courts decided in Lindsay's favor. Backed by corrupt railroad interests, Smith ran again for governor in 1872 and was defeated. Not much more was heard of this strange man.

ROBERT BURNS LINDSAY
(1870–1872)
Colbert County

After the catastrophic term of W.H. Smith, the nadir of Alabama history, the tenure of Robert Burns Lindsay was like a reprieve. His administration made a first step toward the reestablishment of honest state government and a realistic relationship between state and federal government. He was elected on the Democratic ticket.

Lindsay generally appointed good men to local government positions, a tactic made possible only by the departure of so many radicals of the criminal opportunist variety, who had either been bought out or run out by the Klan.

The scandal of the Alabama and Chattanooga Railroad was a mar on his administration but not on Lindsay personally. Soon after his election, the railroad defaulted on payment of interest on its bonds, and the legislature authorized Lindsay to seize the road and pay the interest. A considerable bit of complex maneuvering followed, with the federal government invalidating the purchase which the state had made on the roads for $312 thousand at a bankrupt sale. However, the state wound up extricating itself from the railroad matter entirely in 1876 by surrendering all claims to bondholders and paying $1 million plus interest.

During Lindsay's term, Alabama Polytechnic Institute (later Auburn University) was established and the towns of Gadsden and Birmingham were incorporated.

Born in Lochmaben, Dumfrieshire, Scotland on July 4, 1824, the son of John and Elizabeth McKnight Lindsay, Robert Lindsay was educated at the parochial schools of Scotland and at the University of St. Andrew. He came to the United States in 1844 to visit his brother David, who lived in North Carolina, and decided to remain as a school teacher and law student. In 1849, Lindsay moved to Tuscumbia, Franklin County, Alabama and continued study of law. In 1852, he was admitted to the bar. In 1853, he was elected to the lower house of the legislature and in 1857 to the state senate on the Democratic ticket. He was elected presidential elector on the Democratic ticket in 1860, but being very pro-Union he could not support states' righter Breckinridge and went over to the Douglas ticket.

Although Lindsay fought secession to the end, when it occurred he remained loyal to his state and to the South; he served in Roddy's Cavalry during a portion of the war. He was again elected to the state senate in 1865; and in 1870, he ran on the Democratic Conservative ticket against the incumbent Smith.

Lindsay refused to run a second time, and soon after his retirement from politics he became an invalid. However, he did continue the practice of law sporadically until his death on February 13, 1902.

Lindsay, a Presbyterian, in 1854 was married to Sarah Miller, sister of ex-Governor Winston.

DAVID P. LEWIS
(1872–1874)
Madison County

The election and administration of David P. Lewis represents the last surge of irresponsible Reconstruction government in Alabama. The remnants of the radicals in the state, supported by still present federal troops, the corrupt railroad interests, and even President Grant, made a comeback in 1872 and elected David P. Lewis governor. Lewis, like Smith, had deserted to the federals in 1863. He defeated Thomas H. Herndon of Mobile, Conservative Democratic candidate. There were numerous charges of fraudulence on both sides in the campaign, but Lewis was declared winner.

However, the governor was not happy with a legislature which boasted a Democratic majority. Lewis particularly wanted to see George E. Spencer elected to the U.S. Senate, and in order to accomplish this he formed his own legislature, centered around a group of Republicans who falsely claimed to have been elected. This "Courthouse Legislature" sat for a while simultaneously with the validly elected Democrats known as the "Capitol Legislature." Lewis appealed to President Grant for federal troops to back this claim, and Grant accommodated him "to save the Republicans." Even though the matter was at last referred to the U.S. attorney general and the Democrats won, George Spencer had already been sent to the U.S. Senate by a state senate converted to radical Republican majority.

Aside from this stirring adventure, Lewis' administration was distinguished by doubling taxes and running the public debt up to $30 million.

David Lewis was born in Charlotte County, Virginia in 1820, the son of Peter C. and Mary Smith Lewis. As a child, he moved to Madison County, Alabama and was given a college education. He studied law in Huntsville and was admitted to the bar.

Lewis represented Lawrence County in the Alabama Constitutional Convention of 1861, where he voted against secession but later signed the Secession Ordinance. The convention elected him to the Provisional Congress of the Confederacy, but he refused to serve. In 1863, Governor Shorter appointed him circuit judge; after a short while on the bench, Lewis went over to the federals and remained there until the war's end.

He returned to Huntsville in 1865 and took up the practice of law. Lewis was elected governor in 1872. During his term, the city of Anniston was incorporated, and State Normal College (later Florence State University) and State Colored Normal and Industrial School at Huntsville (later Alabama Agricultural and Mechanical University) were established.

The power of the carpetbaggers and scalawags was entering a decline at this time, and Lewis countered by appointing illiterate Negroes to some minor offices. People, both North and South, at last had grown weary of fraudulence, of terror, of seeing ex-convicts as state officials and ignorant people serving as teachers. But the radicals did not give up their power easily, and the election of 1874 became a bitterly fought one. There was much bribery and wild promises were made to Negroes. Thousands of tons of provisions and food were sent in to "flood sufferers" when there had been no flood, and hundreds of loyal whites were arrested for the duration. The frantic spending became almost comic. According to historian Moore, Lewis' secretary was paid $21 thousand for services in dispensing "political bacon" in the campaign. Grant, consistently displaying a rather primitive intellect, offered to send in troops again, but Lewis (to his credit) refused them.

The election of 1874 was in essence white vs black— it was a contest for reestablishment of white control in the state. Partially because the radical Reconstruction period had sickened reasonable men, the Democratic party in Alabama was victorious. George Houston won over incumbent Lewis by a vote of 107,118 to 93,628.

The Reconstruction period of troop occupation, of oppression and chicanery and hypocrisy, of crime, suffering, and death was at an end.

David P. Lewis retired to his law practice in Huntsville, where he died July 3, 1884. He was never married.

GEORGE S. HOUSTON
(1874–1878)
Limestone County

The inauguration of George S. Houston as governor of Alabama in November, 1874, marked the end of Reconstruction under carpetbag rule and the beginning of the Bourbon or "conservative" period. The tone of state government set by the Houston administration prevailed, almost as an unwritten code, until the 1890s.

Although federal troops were not removed until after the inauguration of President Hayes in 1876, the slow, toilsome effort at a new kind of Reconstruction began in 1874. The main problems confronting the new regime were absolute poverty, bankrupt government, a devastated land, and a race situation which had been aggravated by the machinations of the carpetbaggers and the "Black Republican" Congress for nine unrelenting years.

George Houston was well equipped to take the leadership in such a challenging period. Although he had

Robert Burns Lindsay
1870–1872

David P. Lewis
1872–1874

George S. Houston
1874–1878

Rufus W. Cobb
1878–1882

opposed secession and had even refused to fight in the Confederate Army, he had also refused to take the oath of allegiance to the United States, had supported the Confederacy, and was well thought of by his fellow Alabamians. He was a brilliant stump speaker, a man of integrity and sound common sense, very much the qualities needed at the time. His background of experience included eighteen years service in the lower house of the United States Congress ending in 1861.

George Smith Houston was born January 17, 1811, in Williamson County, Tennessee, son of David and Hannah Pugh Houston. In 1821, the family moved to Lauderdale County, Alabama, where George was educated at the Lauderdale County Academy and read law. He later attended law school in Kentucky. He was admitted to the bar in 1831 and moved quickly into politics. Having become a resident of Limestone County, he was district solicitor several times and was elected to the state legislature in 1832.

In 1841, Houston was elected to the lower house of the U.S. Congress and served there almost continuously until his resignation following secession in 1861. He was consistently opposed to secession. Being a strong Union man, he was elected to Congress as a Unionist candidate in 1850 on the platform that secession was unconstitutional. Houston was graceful in accepting the inevitable, however, and following secession he resigned his congressional seat. He was author of the statement submitted by the Alabama delegation to the Speaker of the House when that delegation departed.

As early as 1849, Houston refused to sign the Calhoun "Address" and denounced it in his campaign for the Senate; however, he ran into much opposition and lost his first Senate race to David Hubbard, a nullification candidate. He was elected to the Senate in 1865, along with ex-Governor Parsons, but like other former Confederates was refused his seat.

Houston, an immensely popular man who became known as the "Bald Eagle of the Mountains," soundly defeated the radical incumbent Lewis for the governorship in 1874.

Whites in the Black Belt helplessly outnumbered by blacks, largely ex-slaves doing the bidding of the carpetbag masters, called on the northern counties to aid in the establishment of the "White Man's Party," and the northern counties responded. *Consolidation* and *union* were words often heard on the hustings. This consolidation so continued (even the name of the party was changed to Democratic–Conservative to appease the Whigs) that in the election of 1876 Houston beat the Republican candidate Noabiah Woodruff by a two-to-one vote.

The Democrats won all seats in the lower house of Congress. In fact, the Republicans carried only eight counties in 1876—six in the Black Belt plus Geneva and Winston (the "Republic of Winston" which had seceded from the Confederacy). And, justifiably or not, the Democrats had learned to manipulate the Negro vote. In this election, they used every means, including intimidation at the polls, to discourage the Republican vote. Whatever the methods, the victory of 1874 meant that home rule was finally restored in Alabama.

In Houston's first term, the Alabama Constitutional Convention of 1875 was held, presided over by General L. P. Walker, with a host of ex-Confederate leaders as delegates. The constitution they wrote provided for "equal political and civil rights to all citizens"; it outlawed loans by state, county, or municipal governments to private business and prohibited the building of railroads by the state government. Many resolutions were voted into law in support of education, but the financial situation forced limits on taxes for education, and the much needed growth of schools was slow. The resolutions provided for the legislature to meet every two years rather than annually and for state elections to be held in August rather than November. The constitution was approved by a popular vote of three to one and became effective in December, 1875.

The four main points of the new constitution, followed assiduously by Governor Houston's administration, were economy, education, payment or abrogation of old Reconstruction debts, and a complete reversal of the practices of Reconstruction. These principles set the tone of every administration afterward into the 1890s.

In his first administration, Houston cut salaries dramatically, eliminated official "deadwood" in state government, and led the debt commission appointed by the legislature in seeking solutions to almost insoluble problems. The greatest challenge was deciding which debts were valid and which were fraudulent. The commission recommended that the state turn over to the creditors first mortgages on the railroads which had defaulted on interest payments. New bonds were issued at a lower rate of interest to substitute for the old carpetbag bonds. The commission report was adopted and $8,596,000 in bonds was issued by the state.

But whatever steps were taken, the healing of the old wrongs—financially, emotionally, and physically—was slow. Alabama continued to stagger under the heavy interest on the old Reconstruction debt for another twenty years; and, as a result, education and any other development requiring state support suffered.

Even so, the public school system was reorganized and the Alabama State Board of Health was established —the first department of public health in the South.

Cullman County was also created. By the end of his second term, Houston had managed to reduce taxes and bring state expenditures under control. A sound if stringent business administration had provided the first steps back toward normalcy.

In 1878, the legislature elected Houston to the United States Senate. Houston died in 1879, while serving his Senate term. He was twice married—to Mary Beatty in 1835 and to Ellen Irvine in 1861.

RUFUS W. COBB
(1878-1882)
Shelby County

Rufus W. Cobb was a close advisor to Governor Houston during the latter's administration. Cobb twice served as state senator (elected in 1872 and 1876), and during his second term he was elected president of that body. He was an able lawyer, industrialist, and cotton planter. His own administration was a relatively quiet one—the federal troops had been withdrawn, the Democrats were in control, and basic work on adjusting the state debt had been accomplished.

Nevertheless, Alabama was growing (population 1,262,505 in the federal census of 1880), and the attendant problems of administrative finance and control of the railroads fell to Cobb. In fact, the problem of regulation of the railroads extended over into O'Neal's administration.

Cobb's administration made extensive improvements in the tax assessment and collection methods. These improvements, together with an efficiently and economically run state government, reduced the cost of government by $40 thousand per year and accumulated a surplus in the treasury of $386,427.

The State Railroad Commission and the State Bar Association were created during Cobb's two terms, and Tuskegee Normal and Industrial Institute (later Tuskegee University) was established.

Rufus Cobb was born February 25, 1829, at Ashville, St. Clair County, Alabama, son of John W. and Catherine Stevens Peak Cobb. His father was a native Virginian who had moved to Abbeville District, South Carolina, and from there to Monroe County, Alabama and later to Ashville.

Young Cobb was educated in the Ashville Academy and at the University of Tennessee, from which he graduated in 1850. He read law in the office of John C. Thomasson in Ashville and in 1855 was admitted to the bar. He practiced law in St. Clair County until he moved to Shelby County in 1867 and became a law partner of B. B. Lewis, later named president of the University of Alabama.

Cobb was twice married—first to Margaret McClung of Knoxville, Tennessee, and second to Frances Fell of Montevallo in 1866. He was a Baptist.

As an industrialist, Cobb served as president of the Central Iron Works at Helena; he was also an attorney for the L&N railroad. He was also one of the developers of an iron mine at Delmar in northern Alabama.

In 1861, Cobb joined the Confederate Army, served as Captain of the Tenth Alabama Regiment, Forney's Brigade, and saw combat service in Virginia. In 1863, he was assigned to General Joseph Wheeler's cavalry then operating in Tennessee.

At the end of the war, Cobb resumed the practice of law, first in Marion, then in Columbiana and Helena. In his second term in the state senate, he collaborated with Peter Hamilton of Mobile on a plan for readjusting the state debt, a plan subsequently adopted by the legislature. He was first elected governor in 1878.

At the end of his second term, Governor Cobb retired to private life but did serve as probate judge of Shelby County to fill the unexpired term of Judge Leeper. Following this service, he moved to Birmingham where he died November 26, 1913.

EDWARD ASBURY O'NEAL
(1882–1886)
Lauderdale County

The period beginning after Governor Houston's administration and extending through some eight governors was a time in which political power rested in the hands of the old Confederate captains. It is doubtful if any man who had not served in the Confederate armed forces and distinguished himself in some way could have been elected to the governorship in these decades. Of this group, none distinguished himself as a soldier more notably than did Edward O'Neal.

After the outbreak of hostilities in 1861, O'Neal enlisted and was appointed major in the Alabama Ninth Infantry. By the following spring, he had achieved the rank of colonel in the Twenty-sixth Alabama Regiment. While commanding this regiment, he was wounded at the Battle of Seven Pines in the Peninsula Campaign. He led Rhodes' Division at the Battle of Chancellorsville where he was again wounded, and he commanded this same division at Gettysburg. In 1864, O'Neal returned with the division to Alabama where it was reorganized and strengthened and sent into the fight against Sherman at Dalton, Georgia; from there, O'Neal commanded forces against the invader at Marietta and Peachtree Creek. Although he never received the commission, he was acting brigadier general at the close of the war.

O'Neal had long been a leader of the Democratic party in northern Alabama, a strong secessionist before the war. He was a member of the Alabama Constitutional Convention of 1875. He had been interested in politics since being admitted to the bar at age twenty-two in 1840. In 1841, he became solicitor of the fourth circuit for four years, and he ran unsuccessfully for Congress in 1848.

O'Neal was a natural choice for governor in 1882 and was reelected in 1884. The principal concerns of his administration seem to have been economy, reduction of taxes, prison reform, and aid to education. The first concern was somewhat marred by state treasurer Vincent's theft of $250 thousand of state funds, an incident which led to O'Neal's establishing the Office of Examiner of Public Accounts and a strong campaign to bring tax collectors in line, many of whom were indifferent and/or corrupt. Several were removed from office, some suits were filed, and in the end a large increase in collections resulted.

The balance in the treasury on September 30, 1883, was $134,418.38; by the end of O'Neal's administration, the balance stood at $286,218.00. In his last two years in office, treasury receipts exceeded disbursements by $340,727.94. At the same time, he succeeded in reducing taxes. Several normal schools were established and considerable increases in appropriations for education were voted by the legislature. The State Department of Agriculture was created, and the University of Alabama received a second land grant from the United States Congress of 46,000 acres to pay for the destruction of the University by Croxton's raiders in 1865. The Board of

Convict Inspectors was established and a thorough study was made of prison conditions with an aim toward meaningful penal reform.

Edward Asbury O'Neal was born September 20, 1818, in Madison County, Alabama Territory. He was the son of Edward O'Neal, a native of Ireland, and Rebecca Wheat O'Neal. The family had moved from South Carolina to Madison County just prior to the birth of son Edward. Edward's father died while the boy was young, and his mother took over the affairs of family and business and tutored her sons.

Edward entered Green Academy, graduated from there, and enrolled in La Grange College from which he graduated in 1836. On April 12, 1838, he married Olivia Moore at Huntsville.

O'Neal studied law, was admitted to the bar in 1840, and began his practice in Florence. At the end of his second term as governor, he returned to Florence where he lived until his death on November 7, 1890.

It seems worth noting that again and again in this period directly following the South's darkest hour men of responsibility, integrity, and unquestioned ability rose to the positions of highest leadership in the defeated and desolate land.

Some modern historians maintain that the Bourbon governors have been overrated, that their concept of government was narrow, that they were so obsessed with the economy and the Negro problem that they neglected to provide those state social services vital to the welfare of the people. Undoubtedly, this is true to some extent, and statistical facts can be produced to prove it. The illiteracy rate among whites and blacks, for instance, was enough to appall the modern reader. Certainly, no one can deny that the basic welfare of the Negro was almost totally ignored. However, given the psychological and emotional terror of the times in the wake of the war and Reconstruction, plus the abject poverty and general physical and material diminution of a whole area, was there some messiah who could have done a better job?

THOMAS SEAY
(1886–1890)
Hale County

Thomas Seay was the twenty-seventh governor of Alabama and third of the "Confederate Captain" governors who followed Houston, reestablishing the Democratic party and white rule in Alabama. Seay followed in the mode established by those governors before him— economy in government, reduction of taxes, and some improvement in education. Seay was a step forward in his particular concern for the welfare of the people, the Negro especially, and in the enactment of social legislation. Moreover, he succeeded in further reducing taxes to only four mills on the dollar, and he left a balance in the state treasury of $200,944.83.

Labor laws were enacted by the Seay administration limiting work periods for women and children to eight hours per day. He established state pensions for Confederate veterans and their widows. New state normal schools were established at Troy (later Troy University) and, for Negroes, at Montgomery (later Alabama State University); and the Alabama Academy for the Blind was opened at Talladega.

Governor Seay was the first of the Bourbons to pay particular attention to the needs of the long neglected Negro population. Following radical Reconstruction, the Negro had been relegated to the position of a sinister alien to be controlled by physical force or paternalism.

Seay expressed his concern for the plight of the blacks and made some small improvement in Negro education and in their general welfare. Booker T. Washington said of him that he was the best friend the Negro ever had. But it was to be a long road from 1886 to the social revolution of the 1960s.

As pointed out, there was little social progress during the Bourbon period. There was, of necessity, considerable neglect of both education and all social services (immense neglect by modern standards), but the first concern was payment of the staggering debt left over from the war and Reconstruction, establishment of state credit, and maintenance of the treasury's solvency. The fact that these financial goals were accomplished is no small tribute to the leaders of this period.

Slowly, the state continued to grow: the census of 1890 showed a population of 1.5 million. Bessemer was founded in 1887, and on March 8, 1888, the first steel manufactured in Alabama came out of the furnaces of northern Birmingham and was rolled at a Bessemer foundry.

Governor Seay was another political leader recruited from the ranks of Confederate war veterans. In 1863, at the age of seventeen, he left his studies at Southern University and enlisted in the Army of the Confederacy. He saw service at the Battle of Spanish Fort and at Blakeley, where he was captured and imprisoned on Ship Island.

Following the war, he returned to Southern University, graduated in 1867, and took up the study of law in the office of Judge A. A. Coleman in Greensboro. He was admitted to the bar in 1869 and began practice as a junior partner in the firm of Coleman and Seay. While practicing law and managing his plantation, he entered politics and was elected to the state senate in 1876. He was twice reelected to the senate and was president of that body when elected governor in 1886.

Thomas Seay was born on November 20, 1846, near Erle, in what was then part of Greene County, the son of Reuben and Ann Green McGee Seay. His father was a native of Georgia and a descendant of a colonial Virginia family. Young Thomas attended rural schools until age twelve, continued his education in the schools of Greensboro, and entered Southern University after graduation.

In 1890, while still governor, Seay entered the race for the U.S. Senate, but was defeated by James M. Pugh. In the turbulent governor's race of 1892, when Reuben Kolb, the Populist, ran against Bourbon candidate Thomas G. Jones, Seay joined other old Bourbon leaders in the fight and insured the election of Jones. But new forces were roaming the political hustings now, and Kolb, as champion of the farmer and the little man, was to bring fear and trembling into the Bourbon camp in the early 1890s. He was never elected governor, but he was the first to challenge the rule of the post-Reconstruction Bourbon order.

Thomas Seay was twice married—first, to Ellen Smaw on July 12, 1865, a native of Greene, later Hale County; and second, to Clara De Lesdernier of New Orleans on March 22, 1881.

Thomas Seay died at Greensboro, Alabama on March 30, 1896.

THOMAS GOODE JONES
(1890–1894)
Montgomery County

In the gubernatorial campaign of 1890, the long, quiet, virtually unopposed rule of the Bourbons ran headlong into its first real challenge. It came in the per-son of Reuben Kolb, so-called champion of the farmer, a Populist, a Jeffersonian Democrat, backed by the powerful Farmers' Alliance. Kolb himself was by background identified with the Bourbons, but he soon pulled away from them, and as commissioner of agriculture built a strong backing among farmers and other low income groups. He soon became one of the most powerful and controversial figures in Alabama politics.

The election of 1890 was exciting and bitter, full of recriminations, charges, and countercharges. Kolb and his followers felt the state Department of Agriculture could do much for the farmer that was not being done. Hard times were upon the country, culminating in the nationwide panic of 1893; prices for agricultural goods were low and freight rates were high. The Kolb people wanted regulation of the railroads, a graduated income tax, direct election of senators, and a secret ballot. They attacked the national banking system, the protective tariff, and screamed for an increase of money and the free coinage of silver.

To his followers, Kolb was a reformer *par excellence,* a man capable of quick change in government for the betterment of the people, in keeping with the larger Populist revolt. To the conservatives, he was an unscrupulous demagogue, ambitious and radical and a danger to the state.

Had Kolb confronted a lesser man, he probably would have won either the first or second election; but Thomas Jones was a powerful figure in Alabama long before he ran for governor. A four times wounded war veteran, he was intelligent, aggressive, and a master speaker on the stump. He represented the epitome of the conservative stance in the state. At the Democratic convention in the summer of 1890, there were three other contestants besides Jones and Kolb. Kolb led in the first thirty-three ballots, but did not obtain a majority. On the thirty-fourth ballot, the delegates of the other three candidates combined with the Jones delegates to defeat Kolb by a vote of 269 to 256. Jones went on to defeat the Republican candidate, B. M. Long, by a landslide vote of 139,912 to 42,390.

Kolb acceded gracefully to his defeat, but after Jones' inauguration, he requested, as commissioner of agriculture, an examination of the books of the Department of Agriculture. Some discrepencies turned up. In the meantime, the legislature passed a law requiring the election of the commissioner of agriculture by the people. There was some confusion as to the date Kolb's term expired. In any case, Governor Jones appointed Herton Lane to serve for the interim between the supposed end of Kolb's term and the elections of 1892. This action lighted the fuse of hatred and vituperation among Kolb's followers and resulted in the bitterest gubernatorial campaign since the election of Houston in 1874.

At the Democratic convention which met on June 8, 1892, both Jones and Kolb claimed a majority of delegates, simply because many counties had sent two delegations. When Jones won the nomination by a vote of 320 to 146, Kolb's delegates walked out to form the Jeffersonian party which Kolb claimed was the real Democratic party. In the election, they carried more counties than did Jones but lost in total votes.

This election in 1892 was a clear fight between the Bourbons and the Radicals. "Jeffersonian Democracy" was the battle cry of Kolb's supporters, and to the man they were opposed to the Democratic machine and the "oligarchy of Bourbonism." They accused the conservatives of being "ballot thieves and stuffers." The Democrats accused them of "conspiring with Republicans, independents, Populists, and the deadly enemies of the Democratic Party in general."

The Alabama Farmers' Alliance had accepted the Ocala platform, adopted in Ocala, Florida in December, 1890, and it became a part of the political issue in the campaign. The Ocala platform was more or less an extension of the old St. Louis platform of the Populists, but it added recommendations for additional government "sub-treasury" action to cover loans on real estate and for government control of public communications and transportation (not ownership). Opposition to this plan raised shadows of the old states' rights issue. There was also much concern among the conservatives about a return to Negro dominance in the state through the alliance.

Jones was attacked for having been attorney for the L&N Railroad and working for the interests of the large corporations against the people. This presaged the later fight Jones, as a federal judge, would have with Governor Comer on the railroad issue.

After the bitter campaign was over, Jones stood the winner by a vote of 11,425. He won most heavily in the Black Belt. Kolb claimed the election a fraud, accusing the Democrats of cheating at the ballot box. Undoubtedly, there was some ballot stuffing, especially in the Black Belt. Even today, there are people in the area who will tell with a wry smile that their grandfathers voted their "bird dogs and long dead relatives."

The legislature had no provision at this time for contesting an election, and it was only through a series of compromises that the Jones victory was finally accepted. This controversy led to the passage of the Sayre Election Law, which required certain educational qualifications for voters and provided for a secret ballot.

Clearly, the people were awake to new issues, and the power of Bourbonism, based on the old issues stemming out of Reconstruction, was on the wane.

But aside from all the bitter conflict, the achievements of Jones' administration were substantial. The Educational Apportionment Act was passed, which provided for appropriation of educational funds to counties on a basis of school population. The Alabama School for Negro Deaf Mutes and Blind (later the Alabama Institute for Deaf and Blind) was established at Talladega. Alabama College (later Montevallo University) was founded and agricultural schools were established at Athens and Evergreen. A complete reform of the convict system was begun, and the legislature finally increased taxation, raising the tax from four to five mills on the dollar.

Thomas Goode Jones was born November 26, 1844, in Macon, Georgia, the son of Samuel Goode and Martha Ward Goode Jones, first cousins; both parents were descendants of colonial Virginia families. While Thomas was still a child, the family moved to Montgomery where Thomas received his early education, augmented by study in two Virginia private academies and finally at the Virginia Military Institute, where he was a student of Stonewall Jackson.

.Thomas left VMI while still a student to enlist in the Army of the Confederacy. He served to the rank of major and saw combat with the Army of Virginia. He was wounded four times and was bearer of the flag of truce at Appomattox.

After the surrender, Jones returned to Montgomery, read law, and was admitted to the bar in 1868. For a while, he was editor of the Montgomery *Daily Picayune*. From 1870 to 1880, he served as reporter for the Alabama supreme court. He was elected to the legislature

Edward Asbury O'Neal
1882–1886

Thomas Seay
1886–1890

Thomas Goode Jones
1890–1894

William Calvin Oates
1894–1896

and was twice speaker of the lower house. In 1866, he was married to Georgena Caroline Bird of Montgomery; he eventually became the father of thirteen children. In 1890, he was elected governor of the state.

Jones was a prominent member of the Alabama Constitutional Convention of 1901, and—along with ex-Governor Oates, Senator John T. Morgan, and others—opposed adoption of the "grandfather clause" and the "good character clause" as unconstitutional requirements to vote.

In 1896, President Theodore Roosevelt appointed Jones to a federal judgeship, where he presided until his death on April 28, 1814.*

WILLIAM   CALVIN   OATES
(1894–1896)
Henry County

William Calvin Oates, another in the line of distinguished war veterans and conservative Bourbons, had been a supporter of Governor Jones in his hard battle with Reuben Kolb. Now, in 1894, with almost fourteen years of service as a U.S. Congressman, he tossed his hat into the ring to run for governor—and against the same formidable opponent, Reuben Kolb.

The issues were the same, but more clearly drawn. The citizens of Alabama were beginning to feel the change in the socio-political winds, and a bitter division in the state was brought on which culminated in the election of Oates and a challenge by Kolb bordering on the threat of civil war.

While Oates' inauguration was taking place on the portico of the capitol, a short distance away down Dexter

*See chapter on Governor Comer for Judge Jones' stand against Comer on the controversial railroad question.

Avenue Kolb had himself sworn in as governor by a justice of the peace. He then gave his own inaugural speech from the back of a wagon to his cheering followers; this done, he led them to the capitol itself and attempted entry. Only calm, decisive action by Attorney General Harvey E. Jones turned them back without bloodshed.

The campaign had been one without precedent in Alabama. Even the churches were divided; there were many fights and some men were killed. The barnstorm type campaigning on the hustings was like something out of a mad dream. The Kolb people adopted the corn cob and the corn cob pipe as their party's symbol—even the mules were adorned with corn cobs; the Oates followers chose a sprig of oats as their insignia. The bitterness had been aggravated by labor strife occurring during Jones' administration, strife which Jones had put down with adamant force. Even the Negro vote was split, with Oates receiving considerable black support from a group led by Bill Stevens, whom the Jeffersonians had offended.

Kolb made the mistake of going to the national Republican party for help, a group eager to break the "solid South." Help came in the meager form of a $5 thousand contribution and considerable lip service. This action only fed ammunition to the Democrats, who harkened back to the days of Republican domination in the Reconstruction. Over and over Oates proclaimed "law and order" to be the crucial issue. Kolb's people claimed he had been counted out in 1890 and 1892, and they did not intend to stand by and see it happen again.

But Oates, like Jones before him, had too much in the old southern tradition going for him. Having lost an arm in battle during the war, he was dubbed "the one-armed hero of Henry County." He not only stood for all the old conservative policies, he personified the southern Democratic leader. When the votes were counted on August 6, 1894, Oates held a majority of 27,000.

Again Kolb claimed he had been cheated and proceeded with his abortive attempt to have himself proclaimed governor. However, he did admit that he lost five counties which he had carried in 1892.

This was Kolb's last stand. Following the election, his political strength dwindled and died, as did the Populist party itself not long afterward. There is something tragic in this dynamic political figure who fought so frantically and with apparent sincerity for the principles and the people he believed in. Needless to say, his principles did not die; they survived to change the shape of the state and the nation after the turn of the century. The New Deal policies of Franklin D. Roosevelt and what has followed since make Kolb's modest proposals seem conservative indeed.

Governor Oates was born November 30, 1835, in Pike (later Bullock) County, Alabama, son of William and Sarah Sellers Oates. The couple had moved from South Carolina to Alabama some years before young William was born. The family was poor and the boy's early education was sporadic. During his teen years, he spent some time in the Southwest working as a carpenter and house painter. Following his return to Alabama, he taught school for about four years while continuing his studies and was able to finance his study of law at Eufala. He was admitted to the bar in 1858; in 1859, he began the practice of law at Abbeville while editing a small Democratic newspaper.

Oates' war record compares with that of Governor Jones. He raised an infantry company in 1861 and served as its captain, within the Alabama Fifteenth Infantry, until 1863. He commanded a regiment at the Battle of Antietam and was promoted to colonel. At the Battle of

Gettysburg, his regiment held the right flank of the Confederate line during the federal assault on Little Round Top. He commanded his regiment at the Battles of Chickamauga and Lookout Mountain. In 1864, he returned to the field in Virginia, in command of the Forty-eighth Alabama Infantry, and lost an arm in battle at Fussel's Mill near Petersburg.

Following the war, he returned to Alabama, resumed the practice of law, and entered politics. Oates was elected delegate to the national Democratic convention in 1868 and to the lower house of the Alabama legislature in 1870. He was chairman of the Judicial Committee at the Alabama Constitutional Convention of 1875. He ran for Congress in 1880 and was elected for the first of seven consecutive terms. On March 28, 1882, he was married to Sallie Toney.

While still in Congress, Oates was elected governor in 1894 and resigned his congressional seat to assume that office. His term as governor was not notable for its achievements, but it was not a time for great achievement. The principal concern was the fight against poverty and the continuing financial depression. But progress was beginning. The first hydraulic generation of electric power was begun on the Tallapoosa River in 1896, and in that same year the first shipment of Birmingham-manufactured iron (75,000 tons) left the port of Mobile for France.

In 1897, Oates tried for the Democratic nomination for the U.S. Senate but lost to General Edmund Pettus of Selma. He served as brigadier general at Camp Meade, Pennsylvania during the Spanish American War.

Oates was elected delegate to the Alabama Constitutional Convention of 1901 where he chaired the Committee on Suffrage and Elections and strongly opposed the "grandfather clause" and "good character clause."

In 1909, he entered the fight over prohibition, opposing the amendment which lost by 25,000 votes.

Oates authored several distinguished articles, a collection of his speeches in the House of Representatives, and *The War Between the Union and the Confederacy,* a book published in 1905.

In his last years, Oates practiced law in Montgomery. His death occurred on September 9, 1910.

JOSEPH FORNEY JOHNSTON
(1896–1900)
Jefferson County

Joseph Forney Johnston ran for the governorship five times; he was successful in 1896 and 1898, serving two consecutive terms. In 1890, he lost the Democratic nomination to Jones; in 1894, he lost it to Oates; in 1902, he lost to the incumbent Jelks. In 1899, he ran for the seat of Senator John T. Morgan unsuccessfully; but in 1907, he was appointed to fill out the Senate term of Senator Pettus, who had died in office. In 1909, Johnston was elected to a full Senate term and so served until his death on August 8, 1913. He served as governor four years and in the U.S. Senate almost six years.

Governor Johnston was something of a political paradox; with aristocratic Bourbon background, he nevertheless adopted some principles of the Populist party and was a free silver man. Actually, Johnston was a moderate progressive and his two terms were, in a sense, a transition between the unsuccessful "radicalism" of Kolb and the highly successful progressivism of Comer, who came like a storm upon the political scene in 1907.

In 1896, Johnston was nominated by the Democratic party and ran against Populist and Jeffersonian candidate Captain A. T. Goodwyn. Johnston was the candidate of the "silver wing" faction of the party, and he had the support of Senators Pugh and Morgan. The Democratic party platform had, in fact, adopted free silver, and Johnston received support from William Jennings Bryan, the young "radical" from Chicago. He even had some Populist support, with many former Kolb men coming over to him. Some of the Populist theory had been accepted by Alabama voters, as well as by the nation; there was much talk of the "haves" and the "have nots" and complaints about the concentration of wealth in the hands of the few. Yet, Johnston, a former bank president and organizer and first president of the Sloss Iron and Steel Works, won the election by 39,000 votes.

In the 1898 campaign, Johnston ran against G. B. Deans, another Populist party candidate; he won heavily. The Populist party was falling apart by this time; improved economic conditions and the acceptance by the Democrats of some progressive measures hastened its demise. Johnston's campaign and election helped to unite the white voters of the state, split between Populist and old-line Democrat.

His two administrations were notable for efficiency, economy, large increases in support of education, and for attracting new industries into the state. Coal mine safety regulations were put into law, and the office of state mine inspector was created. A law was enacted prohibiting children under fourteen and women from working at hazardous jobs. Money was appropriated to build a state boys' industrial school.

Although Governor Johnston opposed it, the legislature passed an additional one mill tax, proceeds to be used exclusively for education. This was the first tax earmarked for education in Alabama history. It was intimated by some that Johnston feared that tax because he had his eye on the Senate seat of Morgan. And in 1899, he did run against Morgan in a spirited race, but failed to unseat the veteran senator. The proposed constitutional convention already authorized by the legislature he considered unpopular and called the legislature into special session to rescind the act, but the vote to revoke failed. Even after the constitution was adopted, Johnston, as champion of the common man, opposed it, stating that it would disenfranchise too many poor white voters.

In his race against Jelks for governor in 1902, Johnston again took the stance as champion of the common man, but lost by approximately 26,000 votes.

The one occurence which marred his administration as governor was his attempt to authorize sale of University of Alabama land to Sloss Steel and Iron Company, with which he had long been affiliated. The sale was contracted at well below market value of the land, but the Board of Trustees for the university refused to approve the sale. Despite all the criticism of Johnston on this matter, no evidence of corruption was ever produced.

Governor Johnston was born in Lincoln County, North Carolina on March 23, 1843, son of Dr. William Johnston and Nancy Forney Johnston. He moved to Alabama at the age of seventeen, attended school at Talladega, but left to enlist in the Confederate Army.

His war record was outstanding. Rising from private to rank of captain in the Twelfth North Carolina Regiment, he served throughout the war; he was wounded four times.

Following the war, Johnston returned to Alabama, studied law at Jacksonville, and was admitted to the bar in 1866. He practiced in Selma but in 1884 moved to Birmingham, a town of 3,000 population. There he practiced law, became president of the Alabama National

Bank, and, along with John W. Johnston, founded and was the first president of the Sloss Iron and Steel Company. In August, 1869, he married Theresa Virginia Hooper of South Carolina.

Johnston was a resident of Birmingham when he was elected governor in 1896. His career spanned as broad a spectrum of active politics as did that of any Alabama governor. He died in Washington, D.C., August 8, 1913, while serving in the U.S. Senate.

WILLIAM JAMES SAMFORD
(1900–June, 1901)
Lee County

Son of a distinguished pioneer Alabama family, a Confederate soldier and officer with an outstanding record, a man of liberal learning and considerable literary and forensic talent, a licensed preacher in the Methodist Episcopal Church South, and a gentleman who in the tradition of his time entered into the public service via elective office, William Samford became the thirty-first governor of Alabama. The tragedy was that Samford had so little time in that high office before death cut short his service.

Born September 16, 1844, at Greenville, Georgia, William was the son of William Flewellyn and Susan Lewis Samford. He attended the private schools of Auburn as a boy and later attended East Alabama Male College (later Auburn University). He enrolled in the University of Georgia, but after less than a year he left, at age seventeen, to enlist in the Army of the Confederacy. He saw combat in the early stages of the war, was promoted to lieutenant, and transferred to Mississippi where he was captured at the Battle of Baker's Creek. He spent eighteen months in the federal prison at Johnson Island on Lake Erie.

However, for the young officer this was no time for brooding upon misfortune. By a stroke of fate, he encountered an old teacher of his, a Professor Slaton, imprisoned in the same stockade, and Samford went back to his studies under Slaton's tutelage. He was released in 1864 and returned to his regiment to serve until the end of the war.

After his discharge from the Confederate Army, Samford was married in October, 1865, to Caroline Elizabeth Drake of Auburn. He continued his studies and began the practice of law in 1867 at Opelika. This was to remain the family home for generations, although Samford during his career did practice law in other southern states, including his native Georgia.

But politics was almost an obligation for the old Confederate captains, and Samford began his political career as alderman of the little city of Opelika. Other offices which he held in succession included delegate to the state Democratic convention, member of the Alabama Constitutional Convention of 1875, and in 1876 alternate presidential elector for the state at large. He served in the Forty-sixth U.S. Congress, 1879–1881; he was elected to the state house of representatives in 1882, then moved on to the state senate where he served two terms, 1884–1888, 1892–1896, and was president of that body for two years. In 1896, he became a trustee of the University of Alabama.

Samford entered the race for governor in 1899 and won the Democratic nomination on the third ballot over four opponents; he was the decided winner in the following general election over Dr. G. B. Crowe.

The question of a constitutional convention came up while Samford was a nominee, and he managed for political reasons to steer away from the suffrage matter. However, after the convention made this a plank in the party platform, he accepted the proposed changes in the suffrage laws, provided nothing in them would disenfranchise white voters.

The Samford legislature voted to submit the matter of the convention to the people, and the voters approved it by a 24,800 majority. The stage was now set for the historic change and the delegates convened in Montgomery on May 23, 1901. Governor Samford died less than a month later on June 10, and the responsibilities of that office, in relation to the convention's decisions, fell to his successor, William D. Jelks.

During his short tenure, Samford laid the groundwork for the establishment of the Alabama Department of Archives and History, appointing the able Thomas Owen to organize and carry it forward.

Among the many honors awarded this Alabama statesman was election to the American Legion of Honor.

WILLIAM D. JELKS
(June, 1901–1907)

When Governor Samford died in June of 1901, after only six months in office, William D. Jelks as president of the state senate automatically moved into the governorship. Jelks was well qualified according to the standards of that day. He was a respected and important figure among the old Confederate captains who for all practical purposes still ran the state, as they did most of the old Confederate South. The outlook was conservative and cautious, primarily concerned with economics and the Negro vote.

The constitution of 1875 was a loose document, and too many of the ills of Reconstruction were intrinsic in it for the white South to bear any longer. The scramble for illiterate Negro votes, the buying and selling of ballots, and the fradulent use of the polls generally had made it mandatory that something be done. The famous, or perhaps infamous, Alabama Constitutional Convention of 1901 was the result.

The planning and even the selection and seating of the 155 delegates in Montgomery on May 23, 1901, came before Jelks was catapulted into the governor's office. But he had been in the state senate, had been its president, had been a major figure in the architecture of the plan, and the long deliberations of the delegates, the final framing of the document, and the vote of the people came while Jelks sat as governor. It was, in fact, the most important accomplishment related to his otherwise rather uninspired administration.

The main purpose of this convention and the constitution it framed and submitted to the people, and which was adopted by a majority vote of 26,879, was to disenfranchise the Negro. Certainly, new and reasonable standards were needed to regulate voting qualifications of both black and white, but the South was still too close to Reconstruction for reasonable steps. Alabama and the nation were to wait over fifty years before realistic measures would be taken under federal pressure to reenfranchise the southern Negro.

The problem which faced the conventioneers was how to completely disenfranchise the Negro without arousing the watchdogs of the federal government in Washington or violating the letter of the U.S. Constitution. It was tricky business, but a solution was arrived at and incorporated into the state document.

First came the residence requirement—two years in

Joseph Forney Johnston
1896–1900

William James Samford
1900–June, 1901

William D. Jelks
June, 1901–1907

Russell McWhortor Cunningham
1904–1905

the state, one year in the county, and three months in the precinct. A second prerequisite to voting would be payment of *all* poll tax due since 1901. The third requirement would be ability to read and write and to read and interpret any chosen part of the U.S. Constitution.

Fourth, applicants must show evidence of regular employment for a better part of the six years preceding the election or must own at least forty acres of land or other property valued at a minimum of $300.00. There then followed a list of crimes for which, if a citizen were convicted, he was ever afterward disqualified.

However, some other provisions, long overdue, were incorporated in the constitution which took the state government forward. Legislative sessions were to be quadrennial in the future rather than biennial; state executive officers were to serve four years rather than two and could not succeed themselves; the office of lieutenant governor was created; and legislative representation was reapportioned by population. Finally, the rate of state property tax was reduced.

It didn't take long for even the less intelligent members of that convention to see that they had disqualified about half the white voting population of Alabama. Something had to be done; and it was. The notorious "grandfather clause" was added and the "good character" clause as well. Any male who had served honorably in the U.S. or Confederate Army, or his lawful descendants, plus men "who are of good character and understand the duties and obligations of citizenship," if properly registered before December 20, 1902, were ever after qualified voters. After that date, all potential voters, white and black, were to be subject to the stringent qualifications drawn up by the convention.

Many Alabamians spoke out against it. Booker T. Washington spoke eloquently against it. The venerable

Senator John T. Morgan, a legend even in his lifetime, strongly opposed the "grandfather clause" as being undemocratic and unconstitutional. Colonel William H. Denson denounced Governor Jelks for proclaiming the new constitution on Thanksgiving Day and called it "the most infamous fraud ever perpetrated upon a people."

One result of this rather wide reaction (generally among poorer whites) to "bossism," and "government by clique," was a demand for a change in the election system from the old state convention to a direct primary. This was enacted into law in 1903. Jelks endorsed it, though rather late.

William D. Jelks was born in Macon County, Alabama but as a child moved to Union Springs in Bullock County. He graduated from Mercer University in Georgia, then returned to his hometown to do newspaper work on the Union Springs *Herald.* He early displayed a marked talent as a writer and soon moved to the larger Eufala *Times,* where he gained a journalistic reputation throughout the state and the southeastern area. He was married to Alice Shorter.

Jelks was elected to the state senate from Barbour County and, with Governor Samford already desperately ill, he was elected president of the senate and next in line for the governorship. He moved into that office at Samford's death in 1901. Jelks finished that term, then ran for the office himself in 1902 and was elected. Due to illness, he was temporarily replaced by Dr. R. M. Cunningham as acting governor for a year in 1904–1905; altogether, Jelks served five years and eight months as governor.

In the 1902 Democratic primary, Jelks was opposed by ex-Governor Joseph F. Johnston who, now outspokenly opposed to the old order, expressed his feeling in the phrase, "the people against the politicians." The new constitution was the great issue; Jelks won by around 26,000 votes, carrying all but four counties.

Jelks' administration was notable for its economy, and he left a surplus in the state treasury of $1.8 million. He was able to effect a five-month minimum school term and create the Alabama Textbook Commission. Child labor legislation was effected in his term, and Houston County (the last county to be incorporated in the state) was created in 1903.

Jelks was a gentleman and a dedicated public servant, but his leadership was not dynamic. The forces whirling about him were not ones which could be stemmed; he followed his legislature in many instances. In a sense, his tenure was a modest rearguard action, the calm which lingered before the furious assault of Braxton Bragg Comer upon much of the staid thinking and governmental orthodoxy of the time.

Jelks died December 14, 1931.

RUSSELL McWHORTOR CUNNINGHAM
ACTING GOVERNOR
(1904–1905)
Jefferson County

Dr. Russell McWhortor Cunningham, a physician as well as a statesman, was born August 25, 1855, at Mt. Hope, Lawrence County, Alabama, son of Moses W. and Nancy Caroline Russell Cunningham. He was educated in the public schools of Lawrence County, and by age seventeen he was teaching school. He used this income, plus money from farming, to pay for his medical education. Cunningham studied medicine under Dr. John M. Clark of northern Alabama, attended the Medical College of Louisville, Kentucky and Bellevue Medical College in New York City. He received his M.D. from the latter in 1879. He became the state prison physician and did valuable work in furnishing statistics on Alabama prison mortality and its causes. He later established a large private practice in Birmingham.

In 1880–1881, Cunningham represented Lawrence County in the legislature. From 1896–1900, he represented that county in the state senate; he was chosen president of that body in 1898. He was a delegate to the Alabama Constitutional Convention of 1901, and later he was elected to the office of lieutenant governor under Governor Jelks. For a year, he served as acting governor during the illness of Governor Jelks. At the end of his term as lieutenant governor, he retired from office* and resumed his medical practice near Birmingham.

Cunningham, professor of medicine at Birmingham Medical College, authored several articles published in medical journals. One of his more notable articles was entitled "Morbidity and Mortality of Negro Convicts."

Dr. Cunningham was married August 13, 1876, to Sue L. Moore, daughter of Judge J. E. Moore of Franklin County. He later wed Annice Taylor of Birmingham. He was a Baptist. He died June 6, 1921, in Birmingham.

BRAXTON BRAGG COMER
(1907–1911)
Barbour County

Braxton Bragg Comer was a man of vision, compassion, courage, and integrity. His achievements, not only during his tenure as governor but also in his colossal business enterprises, provided an enduring stimulus to

*See references under Governors Jelks and Comer for further activity of Dr. Cunningham in politics.

the commercial, social, political, and educational progress of Alabama.

Born in Barbour County, Alabama in 1848, Comer was the fourth son of John F. Comer, former judge of the superior court of Georgia. The Comer family moved from Virginia to Georgia in the early nineteenth century, thence to Barbour County, where the father established a large plantation and lumber business.

It was in this somewhat idyllic way of life that Braxton Comer grew up. He rode, hunted, and fished as a boy; after his father's death, he helped his mother run the plantation. Here he learned the rudiments of business and commerce. Comer told his friends, "It was a joy to be a boy in those days."

As a young man of seventeen, Comer enrolled at the University of Alabama during the last year of the Civil War. There on campus he saw combat as a member of the cadet corps mustered into the Confederate forces to fight a hopeless battle against General Croxton's raiders, who burned the university after forcing the youthful army into retreat.

Following the close of the Civil War, Comer enrolled for further study at Emory, but later transferred to Henry College in Virginia where, after earning an extraordinarily high scholastic record, he received the B.A. and M.A. degrees in natural science.

Upon graduation, Comer returned to Barbour County and took over the management of the plantation, expanding it to 30,000 acres and, even in those trying days, becoming one of the largest and most successful cotton growers in Alabama. In 1872, he married Eva Jane Harris of Cuthbert, Georgia. He was a member of the Methodist Church.

Comer soon moved to Anniston to establish a wholesale grocery and commission business. Five years later, having watched the birth and expansion of industrial Birmingham from afar, he moved his young family to that city. There he purchased the controlling interest of the City National Bank and became its president, only to move rapidly into the cotton manufacturing business by establishing the Avondale Mills of Birmingham in 1897. This industry expanded over the years into one of Alabama's largest cotton manufacturing enterprises. B. B. Comer was one of the first of the big industrialists to create a profit-sharing plan for his employees.

The extravagantly high and usurious freight rates imposed upon the industries and people of Alabama caught Comer's attention and concern in the early years of his industrial enterprises. As was his nature, he acted. This was the moment when he crossed his Rubicon into the arena of political battle and public service. He entered the primaries in 1903, running for president of the Railway Commission. All efforts before this to challenge the power of the railroads had been limited and timid. Comer ran against the incumbent president of the commission, John V. Smith, who had the backing not only of the railroads but of nearly every newspaper in Alabama. Comer immediately endorsed the more liberal Georgia Railway Commission law. He was labeled "radical" and "disturber of the peace"; some papers even pleaded with him to retire from the race "for the good of the State." All old-line politicians opposed him.

But as the campaign proceeded, it became evident throughout the state that a new leader, a new political power, had emerged. The voters heard Comer and believed him, and he won the contest by a large majority. The Montgomery *Journal* termed his victory "a revelation and a revolution."

However, Comer found his hands tied by his associates on the commission in his efforts to carry out his promises; he determined to carry on the fight by entering the gubernatorial campaign of 1906 against Lieutenant Governor Russell M. Cunningham. Cunningham was a master politician and had the political hierarchy of Alabama behind him.

Comer stumped the state, carrying his message of the arrogant, unmindful continuance of unfair freight rates directly to the people. It was one of the bitterest political campaigns in Alabama history but apparently provided exactly the arena of combat in which Comer reveled and excelled. He won a sound victory.

The tide of his victory and the image of his strength swept the progressive wing of the Democratic party into dominance. The legislature was behind him and he lost no time in acting. Proposed measures for change rolled through this normally recalcitrant body.

Among the many progressive laws passed at the governor's bidding was a dramatic series which constituted the railway code. This code prescribed reasonable rates, elimination of all rate discrimination, and adequate public service in all forms, and defined the methods and powers by which the commission was to enforce the new rules.

But the railroads were not to be stopped totally at this point. They took the law to the federal district court in Montgomery, presided over by Judge Thomas G. Jones, ex-governor, who held the railway code to be unconstitutional and issued a temporary injunction against its enforcement. Comer countered with a special legislative session and adoption of the new "injunction-proof code." Jones answered with a court order designed to prevent all public officers from taking action against the railroads under the new code. Comer appealed to the federal circuit court in New Orleans. This court ruled in his favor, so the railroads appealed to the Supreme

Court of the United States. There the battle came to an end with a judgment declaring the code constitutional and just. On June 1, 1901, the new rates went into effect.

Comer did not rest long after this battle. His next assault was upon tax assessment regulations, which he considered unfair and even discriminatory. This conflict also involved the railroads, which had long received favorable treatment. Comer set up the Alabama Tax Commission and state Board of Equalization to "equalize property values and to tax all property at the proscribed 60% of value." Assessed values of property in the state immediately increased, as did property tax monies.

Comer, despite his hard and combative exterior, seems to have been a compassionate man with the interests of the less fortunate in mind. Among laws and executive orders put into effect were increases in Health Department funds, creation of a tuberculosis sanitorium, state supervision of the Boys' Industrial School, a child labor law which among other provisions made it illegal to hire any child under twelve years of age to work in cotton mills and provided some measure of compulsory school attendance.

Comer also made massive reforms in the Alabama penal system and set up a cotton mill industry within the state using convict labor. He appointed H. H. Stewart II, a cotton mill executive from Selma, as manager of the small mill at Speigner prison in 1909. From this modest beginning, Stewart developed a cotton manufacturing industry for the state which, over a period of forty years, would provide a large part of the support for the Convict Department, would furnish all clothing and bedding for the inmates, and would give them regular employment. With the construction of Kilby Prison in 1923, a large additional cotton mill was included and a national and international market for the convict-made chambries was created. Comer's foresight and understanding of the needs of the prison system made this gigantic enterprise a massive savings to the taxpayers of the state for nearly half a century.

But perhaps Governor Comer has been lauded most for his contributions to the educational system of Alabama, which won him the title of the "educational governor." The strides made during his four years in office were indeed giant ones. Appropriations for schools and institutions were increased by millions. The new county high school system was established, with high schools being erected in every county except those possessing a district agricultural school or a state teachers' college. The whole curriculum was examined and improvements adopted.

Comer's only failure seems to have been his attempt to establish prohibition in Alabama.

Governor Comer retired at the end of his term in 1911, but feeling the call once more to combat reactionary forces, he ran again in 1914. But this time, in a run-off primary, the conservative forces beat him. At the death of Senator J. H. Bankhead in 1920, Comer was appointed by Governor Kilby to serve the remaining period of the Bankhead term. After this last public service, Comer retired to run his business interests which he continued successfully until his death in 1927.

EMMETT O'NEAL
(1911–1915)
Lauderdale County

Governor Emmett O'Neal represented the best characteristics of the legendary "southern gentleman"; a certain sense of *noblesse oblige* seemed to move him into service of the state.

As governor, O'Neal was hampered by a legislature which balked at many of his progressive proposals, and he was crippled by scandals growing out of theft and misappropriation of funds by lesser officials within his administration. But he was one of the giants, and his administration was a meaningful one to Alabama.

The paradox is that he was considered a conservative as opposed to "radical" Comer. This view may have grown in part from Comer's uncompromising attack upon the railroads and his "revolutionary" tax proposals. As a matter of fact, O'Neal was a man more ahead of his time both in political philosophy and in action than was Comer. Under the skin, they were made of much the same stuff. Their major difference politically was on the prohibition issue.

Emmett O'Neal was born September 23, 1853, at Florence, Alabama, son of future governor Edward A. O'Neal and his wife Olivia. He was one of the most thoroughly educated men ever to serve as governor of Alabama. After early training in the preparatory schools of Florence, Emmett attended and graduated from Florence Wesleyan University. He continued his education at the University of Mississippi, 1870–1871, and later at the University of Alabama. He studied law in his father's law office and was later admitted to the practice of law in Alabama by Judge William Wood. He became his father's law partner, an affiliation which continued until the senior O'Neal's election to the governorship in 1881. In that same year, Emmett married Lizzie Kirkman of Florence.

In 1884, young O'Neal was elected a presidential elector and canvassed the state in support of the Democratic party, proving himself an impressive orator. O'Neal's talents as a speaker kept him constantly on call. His reputation became nationwide. His address "Representative Government and Common Law," delivered to the New York State Chamber of Commerce, was so scholarly and so effective that Congress printed it as a public document. In 1892, O'Neal was chosen presidential elector from the state at large; and in 1893, Grover Cleveland appointed him United States district attorney.

O'Neal was prominently active in the Alabama Constitutional Convention of 1901, chairing the committee on local legislation. He supported William Jennings Bryan for the presidency on the Democratic platform in 1908 and stumped several far western states on behalf of his candidacy.

He heartily opposed the proposed prohibition amendment of 1909 which would have made Alabama totally dry, suggesting instead a local option. O'Neal was largely responsible for the failure of the prohibition amendment, and Comer never forgot the defeat at the hands of this suave, polished and articulate foe. O'Neal was tagged a conservative, yet on this issue he was far more progressive than Comer.

After serving as president of the Alabama Bar Association, Emmett O'Neal at the age of fifty-seven was elected governor of Alabama in 1910. Like Comer, O'Neal understood the overwhelming needs of education in the state, and he set out early in his administration to fill those needs. Unlike Comer, he did not have the full backing of his legislature, and his undertakings were never entirely achieved. He did, however, improve education overall, and through legislative act increased educational appropriations heavily; only the difficulties resulting from the failure of his tax revision proposals attenuated these appropriations. O'Neal succeeded in creating the Alabama rural library system and in setting up a board of trustees for the several state normal schools.

In other areas, O'Neal succeeded in progressive measures. He created the Alabama Highway Commission and the Oyster Commission. He sponsored laws for better protection of miners and for improved child labor regulation (he was, unhappily, never granted all he wished in this area). The Alabama court of appeals was created, which helped to relieve the backlog of cases pending before the U.S. Supreme Court. After several local bank failures, O'Neal proposed and was granted power to organize the state Banking Department, primarily for the purpose of supervising banking procedures and enforcing the banking laws.

Some of the progressive measures which Governor O'Neal proposed and which the legislature turned down may make the whole process of democratic government seem to the modern reader incredibly ponderous, slow, and ineffective. Among the defeated proposals were a driver's licensing law, requiring driver tests at the wheel; allowance of a special school tax; reform of municipal government; complete reorganization of the state's public school system in the name of economy and efficiency; and revision of the criminal code to expedite prosecution of criminals and remove long delays which so often obstructed justice. O'Neal was also hamstrung in improving workmen's compensation laws and child labor laws, already initiated under Comer. Finally, he was turned down in his effort to establish a Public Utilities Commission. Indeed, in view of these frustrating acts of the legislature, it seems a mystery that he was able to effect passage of a local option liquor law to apply throughout the state.

O'Neal's tenure as governor was further hampered by thefts of public monies occurring within the state Convict Department, headed by James G. Oakley, and within the Department of Agriculture. Minor officials in both departments were tried, sentenced, and served terms in prisons for the crimes. Oakley was tried and found not guilty on the charge of misuse of state funds. However, the prolonged and ugly scandal, touted almost daily by the newspapers, weakened the effectiveness of O'Neal's administration. There was never any question but that O'Neal was free of any involvement in these crimes.

After O'Neal left office in 1915, he was appointed a federal referee in bankruptcy and served in Birmingham, Alabama. In 1920, he entered the Democratic primaries for election to the U.S. Senate but was defeated by J. Thomas Heflin.

Governor Emmett O'Neal, labeled conservative, was one of the most liberal men of his time. Under different circumstances, he might have been one of the state's great governors. He died September 7, 1922.

CHARLES HENDERSON
(1915–1919)
Pike County

Governor Charles Henderson labeled himself a conservative and promised in his campaign for the governorship to pursue "conservative business methods." He kept his promise and as a result was able, with a cooperative legislature, to turn the state's financial deficit into a surplus and to liquidate most of the outstanding debts. He also succeeded in enacting into law some of the fine proposals made by O'Neal, who supported him for governor.

The second half of Henderson's term saw a rapid upsurge in the economy due to America's entry into World War I. This trend, together with Henderson's strict business methods and additional income from his tax equalization measures, brought the state's financial status to its strongest level since the Civil War.

Charles Henderson was born April 26, 1860, in the community of Henderson, Pike County, Alabama. He was the son of Jeremiah Augustus and Mildred Hill Henderson. His early education was in the schools at Troy; in 1875, he entered Howard College, then located at Marion, Alabama. Due to the death of his father, he left Howard before graduation and returned home; he began his business career at the age of seventeen.

Henderson later became director of Troy Compress Company and of the Farmers and Merchants National Bank of Troy. He was elected mayor of Troy for seven different terms and served a total of thirteen years in this capacity. He was one of the founders of Troy State Normal College and was inspector general on the staff of Governor William J. Samford. He was married to Laura Parker.

In 1906, Henderson was elected to the Railroad Commission, was made its chairman, and was then re-elected to this position twice, in 1908 and 1912. In that memorable fight between Governor Comer and the railroads, Henderson was a calm and moderating influence which finally brought a modicum of understanding to both sides.

When he entered the governor's race in 1914, Henderson's severest contest was in the Democratic primary run-off against Comer. This he won, with the able help of ex-Governor O'Neal, who was infuriated by Comer's attacks on the records of O'Neal's administration. Here again, the opposing wings of the Alabama Democratic party clashed. Prohibition again was an issue, with Henderson upholding local option and Comer proposing the prohibition of all alcoholic beverages. In the general state elections of November, Henderson easily won against a trio—John Shields, Republican; E. H. Cross, Progressive; and W. C. Swain, Socialist. Henderson was inaugurated January 18, 1915.

But even after his victory, the prohibition forces were not stilled; they controlled the legislature which passed a bill to reinstate prohibition, submitting the bill to O'Neal on his last day in office. He ignored it, and after the inauguration, Henderson promptly vetoed it. However, the legislature succeeded in passing the bill over his veto, killing his amendment for a popular referendum. Thus, prohibition was at last thrust upon Alabamians under what became known as the "bone dry" law of 1915. Consequently, Alabama was a dry state before the federal prohibition amendment, the eighteenth, was ratified under the Kilby administration. The state remained dry from 1915 to 1933 when the Twenty-first Amendment to the Constitution, repealing prohibition, was ratified. Both Comer and Kilby, two of Alabama's greatest governors, could not foresee the horrors which such an unenforceable law would bring down upon the country.

In the second, more prosperous half of his administration, Henderson asked for, and was granted by the legislature, additional taxes. After learning that 40 percent of Alabama recruits examined were physically unfit, he supported the Health Department's efforts for improvement of public health regulations and enactment of additional health laws.

In 1915, the legislature passed the Consolidated Court Bill, designed to reform the court system, mainly by abolishing local courts and consolidating their functions in district courts. However, certain amendments were not included in the bill that Henderson felt were imperative, and he refused to sign it. His administration continued to gather information regarding the courts

Braxton Bragg Comer
1907–1911

Emmett O'Neal
1911–1915

Charles Henderson
1915–1919

Thomas E. Kilby
1919–1923

and the judicial system which laid a basis for future court reform.

With the able assistance of William F. Feagin, state superintendent of education, he made progress with the educational system. Fifteen major laws were passed to bolster public education in Alabama. One of these dealt with a problem of frightening proportions—illiteracy. One out of twelve whites was illiterate, one out of four Negroes. An Illiteracy Commission was formed and its work incorporated into the educational system. Financing of education was stimulated by a law giving local option authority to county and school districts to levy an additional three mill tax for education. A compulsory school attendance law was passed in 1915.

The primary election laws were amended to systematize the primary election code and render the procedure less liable to corrupt political activity.

Henderson made considerable effort to improve the penal system, including a recommendation that all convicts be kept at the Speigner prison rather than in scattered, unimproved camps all over the state, and that they be employed on the state farms and in the Speigner cotton mill.

The one-crop system in the South had become a crippling force upon agriculture. Henderson stumped the state in an effort to convince farmers they must break with the one crop (cotton) system and diversify. This was the first major step in Alabama toward what would become a revolution in all southern agriculture.

Henderson's administration was a successful one, particularly in fiscal matters; and it was success achieved in spite of the distraction, disruptions, and burdens of a world war. When he came into office, the budget deficit was $450 thousand. By 1918, he had transformed this to a $675 thousand surplus. Governor Henderson fulfilled his pledge to make good business administration the foremost of his official priorities.

He died January 7, 1937.

THOMAS E. KILBY
(1919–1923)
Calhoun County

Thomas E. Kilby of Anniston, Calhoun County, Alabama might be evaluated by any criteria as one of Alabama's ablest governors. He was an experienced and astute businessman and brought these practical talents to the governorship, enabling him to achieve what most politicians merely talk about—increased income, a regulated process of all state expenditures, and a balanced budget during most of his term.

Kilby was sober, scrupulously honest, independent, and steady. He looked upon government as intrinsically a business matter involving first of all the careful, wise handling of monies. But the social and educational measures made into law during his administration stand as strong evidence that he was also a man with a social conscience. He did not have the impelling personality or fiery force of Comer, the intellect of Emmett O'Neal, or the articulate brilliance and rhetorical powers of Dixon; but he was a man of strong character, impeccable integrity, and sober intelligence.

Kilby was born in Lebanon, Tennessee on July 9, 1865, the son of Peyton and Sara Ann Marchant Kilby. His father, a native of Wilkes County, North Carolina, lived for a number of years in Atlanta, Georgia where young Kilby received his early education in the public schools. The family moved to Anniston when Thomas was a young man. Here he soon proved himself a capable businessman.

Kilby first became agent of the Georgia Pacific Railroad; then in 1899, with Oscar E. Smith, he organized and operated Kilby Locomotive and Machine Plant. In 1905, he was made president of the City National Bank of Anniston. From 1900 to 1905, he was an active member of the Board of Education of Anniston, and from 1905 to 1909 he was Anniston's progressive mayor. Kilby succeeded not only in improving the financial situation of the city but also in its landscaping, fostering architectural projects which so improved the looks of Anniston that it was given the sobriquet "Model City." He was married to the former Mary Elizabeth Clark.

In 1911, Kilby was elected to the state senate where he served until his 1914 election as lieutenant governor of Alabama.

When Kilby tossed his hat into the ring for the governorship in 1918, there were four other candidates in the race. The three principals were Kilby, William W. Brandon, and Charles B. Teasley. The campaign was relatively quiet, certainly lacking the combativeness and personal vituperation which characterized the race of 1907. The main issue seems to have been the proposed prohibition amendment to the federal Constitution. Kilby was a stout prohibitionist and immediately received the endorsement of the Anti-Saloon League. He also had the support of Alabama's leading newspapers. Kilby ran his own campaign, indebting himself to no large financial contributors. When he took office, he felt himself to be unfettered and had the prohibitionist legislature solidly behind him.

His inauguration was one of the gala political and social occasions in Montgomery. World War I had just ended and people quite possibly felt that a new era was dawning, as in fact it was, but not so peaceful and idyllic as they believed.

In setting out to keep his campaign promises, Kilby chose first the matter of prohibition. As expected, the amendment passed overwhelmingly. Alabama, already dry, became one of the first states to ratify what would turn out to be the most abysmal failure in American legislative history.

Of the many improvements and changes in the state which Kilby was to propose, the first, of necessity, was a method to pay for the rest. Thus he established an effective state budget system. This dealt largely with the system for disbursement of state funds, but his legislature also passed additional taxes—a graduated income tax, a severance tax on all coal mines in Alabama, and higher, more equitable assessments of all property.

After these basic budget measures, first in line of importance was the tremendous improvement of the educational system. A state Board of Education was created, and the increase in appropriations for elementary and high schools was the highest in the state's history, $6,653,563 more than the total appropriations in Henderson's administration.

Now that he had begun, Kilby moved forward without pause—he created the state Child Welfare Department, monitored passage of workmen's compensation laws, increased appropriations by millions to the Public Health Department, bulldozed through the legislature a $25 million road bond issue with an amendment appropriating $10 million for badly needed improvements at the port of Mobile, established a home for retarded children, created the state Law Enforcement Department, and strengthened law enforcement generally. It was also during Kilby's tenure that the amendment to the state constitution ratifying the Nineteenth Amendment to the federal Constitution was passed into law—women's suffrage.

Finally, one of the crowning achievements of Kilby's administration was the erection of the ultra modern Kilby Prison, including a new 20,000-spindle cotton mill to add to the old Speigner mill which had long proven the efficacy of profit-making industries within the penal system. Kilby Prison opened its institutional doors in 1923.

Kilby ran for the Senate in 1926 and in 1932 but was both times defeated by Hugo Black, who later became a justice of the U.S. Supreme Court.

After these two defeats, Kilby retired from active politics. He died October 22, 1943.

WILLIAM W. BRANDON
(1923–1927)
Tuscaloosa County

"Plain Bill" Brandon, as this governor was affectionately called, was not so plain. He was an astute and cunning politician, with a charm and physical appearance which appealed to his constituents. His neatly trimmed, greying mustache, his mane of carefully brushed hair, his plain (though expensive) clothes, and a naturally warm southern manner which he could direct toward any level made him a politician's politician. He was small of stature but had a powerfully resonant voice.

William W. Brandon was born June 5, 1868, in Talladega, the son of Reverend and Mrs. Frank Brandon. His early education was at Cedar Bluff Institute and Tuscaloosa High School. A young man of extraordinary energy and enterprise, he went to work for himself at age thirteen and helped defray the costs of his education.

After attending the University of Alabama Law School, he began law practice at Tuscaloosa in 1892, having served as city clerk in 1891. He had the southerner's penchant for military glory and became a major in the Third Alabama Volunteer Infantry Regiment during the Spanish American War.

Brandon served two terms in the Alabama house of representatives—1896–1897 and 1898–1899. He served as state adjutant general from 1899 until 1906 and reorganized the old Alabama National Guard. He served as state auditor from 1907 to 1911. In 1911, he was elected probate judge of Tuscaloosa County. He was married to the former Elizabeth Andrews Nabors.

Brandon moved with steady consistency up the political ladder in Alabama. By 1918, he was well known over the state and he was ready to run for governor. He had identified himself with the indomitable Comer. The main competitors in the race were Kilby and Teasley, both of whom had strong newspaper support. Brandon maneuvered himself between these two and drew off thousands of votes. In the final count, he was within 3,404 votes of Kilby's total.

As Brandon himself stated, he "hit the ground running" after that defeat. By 1922, he was a strongly backed candidate. He defeated Bibb Graves (making his first run) by an overwhelming majority of more than three to one.

The principal plank in his platform seems to have been economy without new taxes, and in this he succeeded. By the end of the fiscal year, September, 1926, the state treasury boasted a surplus and the outstanding state debts had been liquidated. Brandon also repealed the tax exemption for the Alabama Power Company, a sizable income source.

Brandon's accomplishments were many. He improved the state highways, using money procured by the Kilby administration; he modernized, in some ways, the state Highway Department; he sponsored passage of the first state law providing a dignified monetary assistance to the aged; he purchased property near the capitol in Montgomery which later provided office space for a growing state government; and, most important, he created the Alabama State Docks Commission, and a $10 million bond issue was sold to finance improvements at this vital shipping point. This was to prove in the ensuing years a meaningful savings to Alabama shippers and was, in a sense, the first stride forward in developing the facilities at Mobile into a major world seaport.

Brandon did little, comparatively, for education in Alabama. There was virtually no increase in state educational appropriations during his administration. It was left to the counties and municipalities.

Evidently, after the strides of the Kilby administration, the people were ready for a more simplistic state government. This Brandon provided. The great vision and intrepid force of character which mark the giants of statesmanship were not Brandon's. His accomplishments were solid, but "Plain Bill" was not one of Alabama's great governors.

He died December 7, 1934.

BIBB GRAVES
(1927–1931; 1935–1939)
Montgomery County

Bibb Graves, descendant of Alabama's first governor and the first Alabama governor in the twentieth century to be elected to two terms, was a man who stood like

William W. Brandon
1923–1927

Bibb Graves
1927–1931
1935–1939

Benjamin Meek Miller
1931–1935

Frank Murray Dixon
1939–1943

collossus, his feet planted on the opposite foundations of a new progressivism and a close association with the most reactionary terrorist organization ever to appear in America, the Ku Klux Klan.

The time was one of radical change, of excitement, when the South was beginning to emerge with a new strength from its long period of deprivation and economic inferiority following the Civil War and Reconstruction. It was a period of reactionary movements. Because the time itself was a paradox, political hopefuls, political leaders, and even political greats inevitably presented paradox in themselves.

Bibb Graves was Grand Dragon of the Alabama Klan when he was elected governor. He was, of course, several cuts above the average Klan member of the time; and he never approved of nor participated in their violence; but he needed their votes, and he became a part of the organization.

But later in his first administration, Graves paid for his membership with cold sweat. The Klan felt its power, the power of its secrecy and its numbers and its self-righteous code of white Anglo-Saxon Protestantism; and like most such organizations led by ignorance and feeding on fear and cruelty, it ran amuck. It felt itself above the law of the land. The KKK dealt out punishment at will, usually in the form of floggings of chosen victims. Nobody, particularly those among the underprivileged, was safe. The citizenry as a whole became sickened, and a few dared to speak out and take up the fight.

Attorney General Charles McCall resigned his position, strapped on two guns, and stumped the state against the Klan. Grover C. Hall, Sr., editor of the Montgomery *Advertiser,* led the fight with uncompromising, courageous editorials, writing with such power and rhetorical splendor that in Alabama the Klan retreated slowly before his attack. He received the Pulitzer Prize for his journalistic efforts in 1928.

Graves himself, although he prompted his law enforcement agencies to crush violence and lawlessness wherever it was encountered, never took the leadership in this fight. However, on February 24, 1928, the Montgomery *Advertiser* announced that Governor Graves had quit the Klan.

Bibb Graves was born at Hope Hull, Alabama in Montgomery County on April 6, 1873. One of Alabama's best educated governors, he attended the University of Alabama, University of Texas, and Yale. He received degrees in engineering and law.

As a young Yale law graduate, he set up a practice in Montgomery, but even then his eye was fixed upon the arena of politics. On October 10, 1900, he married Dixie Bibb, a cousin from Montgomery. Dixie was later appointed to fill out Hugo Black's Senate term when he was appointed to the Supreme Court.

Graves was elected first to the state house of representatives and later became chairman of the Alabama Democratic Executive Committee. In World War I, he served as a colonel and was for many years active in the Alabama National Guard and the American Legion. The American Legion, organized labor, and the Klan supported him solidly in the 1926 election, which he won, over the opposition of all major newspapers, with a vote of 83,472 to 74,153 for A. H. Carmichael, his nearest opponent.

Actually, Graves represented the progressive forces, recommending a continuation of the Kilby administration policies and a furthering of needed aid to educational and social services. The conservative candidate was Lieutenant Governor Charles S. McDowell, Jr. of Eufala, who was backed by the Brandon forces. Everyone shouted better highways; McDowell proposed a $75 million highway bond, while Graves proposed an issue of $25-35 million.

Graves began his first term with a legislature whose majority had not supported him in the race. But the progressives were behind him, and when his measures proved popular, the legislature gradually began to follow, endorsing his proposals consistently.

For action, there had never been anything like the first Graves administration. The legislature of 1927 passed 700 bills, largely progressive legislation in tune with the political and social philosophy of the governor.

In special session, the legislature passed a constitutional amendment, submitting to the people a decision on a $25 million road bond issue. A two-cent gasoline tax was passed to defray interest and help retire the principal on the bonds.

The largest single appropriation for education in Alabama's history was passed, funding the public school system with $600 thousand. The bill also included a measure to extend the school term to seven months.

The Highway Department was organized, and the convict lease system was abolished. Convicts who had previously been leased to private interests were put to work on the public highways.

A corporation was formed by the state to raise money for construction and operation of fifteen toll bridges. Without question, Bibb Graves constructed more highway bridges than any other governor of Alabama; several of them were named for him.

A $5 million bond issue was approved for improvement of the docks and shipping facilities at Mobile and some inland docks.

In educational measures, the legislature was stumbling over itself in an effort to improve and bring Alabama schools up to date. The Brown Textbook Bill, an effort to improve not only the texts, but also the procedures for their sale and distribution, was passed. And just before the legislative recess, the munificent Ward Bill, proposing a $17 million appropriation for education, was introduced; it passed after the legislature reconvened.

Perhaps the most controversial bill during Graves' two terms was the Tunstall Revenue Bill. In spite of Graves' platform, the bill was passed by the legislature calling for a 15 percent tax on cigars, cigarettes, and tobacco. A storm broke over the governor's head; he was severely criticized for breaking faith with the little man. And as a sample of the strong legislative leadership Graves could assert, he collared the leaders of the senate, formed a committee, and told them what changes he wanted. The committee became known as the "Graves Steamroller." Within a short time, the original bill was changed beyond recognition. Tax burdens were switched to railroads, telegraph and telephone companies, coal, iron, and other industry. The bill passed with a good majority. Graves rode out that storm successfully.

The Alabama Motor Carrier Act, a needed law, placed all commercial highway vehicles under the control of the Public Service Commission.

With all this progressive legislation and skillful guidance by Governor Graves, some incredibly reactionary bills were introduced concurrently. An anti-evolution bill, similar to that of Tennessee, was fortunately defeated. The Frey "press muzzling" bill was defeated only by the tactic of the senate's sudden adjournment. And then, a strong anti-masking bill, directed at the Klan, was defeated. However, a bill providing strong legal punishment for "flogging while masked" was substituted and passed; apparently it was permissible to flog without a mask.

Next to educational measures, the greatest achievement of the first Graves administration was in the field of public health. Modern health services were rendered to a larger proportion of the population in Alabama than in any other state in the Union.

Industrial growth and development in the state was sponsored by Graves and resulted in a mushrooming of factories, industrial output, and increased payrolls. At the end of Graves' first term, Alabama was well on the way to overcoming the poverty and wounds of the past.

The difficulty was that appropriations did not keep pace with incoming funds. When Graves' term ended in January, 1931, the public debt was over $15 million. The period of deficit spending had begun.

The 1934 gubernatorial campaign in Alabama, in which Graves ran against Judge Leon McCord and Frank Dixon, was exciting and colorful. Graves was up against formidable opponents. McCord was a silver-tongued orator who, it was said, made more people weep and more people laugh than did any other politician in Alabama history. Frank Dixon, new on the political horizon, was intelligent, educated, and bent on modern reform. He was a brilliant speaker, a veteran who had lost a leg on the fields of France, handsome, patrician, and aggressive.

Outside of Dixon's revolutionary platform, there was little difference in the several proposals of the candidates. Graves had his organization and was a canny politician with the full support of labor. In the primary, he led Dixon, his nearest opponent, by almost 35,000 votes. In the June run-off in which Dixon introduced the slogan "new against the old order," Graves won with 157,240 votes to 135,309 for Dixon. The close vote shook the old-line politicians in Alabama.

Graves' second term was not so noteworthy or marked by such remarkable legislative advances as was his first. The nation had passed into the hardships of the Depression, and much of what the state government accomplished was in the nature of cooperation with federal relief projects. Alabama was said to have its own New Deal. Relief funds for the state were increased bountifully and development was continued on the TVA project with its great dams and lakes on the Tennessee. In this same period, the landmark ruling of the Supreme Court gave undisputed legal authority to this government-owned project to manufacture and sell electrical power.

The state Department of Labor was organized and labor became a potent force, paralleling its rise in strength nationally. A Department of Public Welfare was created in 1935, and the Alabama State Employment Service, partially funded with federal monies, was set up to help alleviate the unemployment situation in the state and dispense unemployment insurance monies, a modest beginning of the vast Social Security structure throughout the nation today.

The bridge tolls over the state, instigated in Graves' first term, were removed. And the prohibition issue was settled at last. The 1937 legislature passed a local option law which Governor Graves signed. It gave each county the right to decide whether it would remain dry or vote itself wet.

Bibb Graves' accomplishments as governor were superior. No other governor before him accomplished so much in providing funds for necessary public services; no other governor since the Civil War or Reconstruction governed so long during such radically changing conditions locally and nationally. The state, the nation, the world were a different dwelling place for man in 1939 than they had been when Graves took office in 1927. In the vital course of these vast changes, Bibb Graves played his part well.

He died on March 14, 1942.

BENJAMIN MEEK MILLER
(1931–1935)
Wilcox County

Sandwiched in between the two terms of the dynamic Bibb Graves, caught in the paralyzing grip of the Depression, the administration of Benjamin Meek Miller seems a bit colorless. And indeed, except for his stubborn fight to adopt a state income tax and his equally stubborn refusal to adopt a state sales tax, Miller's time in office was pallid. Nevertheless, some stabilizing laws were introduced during his term which have become part of the fabric of Alabama state government.

Governor Miller was born on March 13, 1864, at Oak Hill in Wilcox County, Alabama, the son of the Reverend John and Sara Miller. As a boy, he attended the schools of Oak Hill and Camden and received his B.A. degree from Erskine College in South Carolina in 1884. For a few years after graduation, he was principal of a high school but soon made the decision to enroll in the law school of the University of Alabama. While he was still a student there, he ran for and was elected to the state house of representatives from Wilcox County and served 1888–1889.

Immediately after graduating from law school and being admitted to the bar, Miller began a law partnership with his brother which lasted off and on for many years and gave the young lawyer firsthand knowledge of the people and their problems which was to prove invaluable in his later political life.

In 1904, he was elected judge of the fourth judicial circuit and in 1921 was elected to an associate judgeship on the Alabama supreme court. Miller was defeated for this position when he ran for reelection in 1927, and he returned to Camden and resumed the practice of law with his brother. Three years later he entered the state primaries of 1930 for the Alabama governorship.

His strongest opponent, out of five, was W. C. Davis. All candidates came out for the usual things—no additional taxes, improved public health and child welfare, and better highways. However, Miller, from an old Black Belt, Presbyterian family and a man of impeccable integrity and high ideals, launched an immediate and vigorous attack on the Klan and on extravagance in state government—a blow to the Graves record and his political forces. Miller beat Davis, his nearest opponent, by over 9,000 votes and in the run-offs was opposed by Judge Hugh Locke who had strong Klan support.

However, Locke (like Tom Heflin who was running for the Senate against John Bankhead) had been read out of the Democratic party after bolting during the Al Smith–Herbert Hoover presidential campaign in 1928. It was almost like old times for a while, and when the votes were in, Miller was winner by over 4,000 votes. Bankhead also beat Heflin for the Senate. This marked, more or less, the last breath of the political power of the Klan in the 1920s.

But the campaign was nothing compared to the grave problems which confronted the new governor when he took office in 1931. The state was deeply in debt, revenues running far below income, and schools were in danger of closing. Miller's immediate, makeshift remedy was to borrow approximately $500 thousand from the banks with 4½ percent public bonds as collateral; previous borrowing by the Graves administration of over $1 million was necessarily included in the new debt.

Miller also instigated early in 1931 a study of the state debt and spending methods generally by the famous Brookings Institute, which finally reported the staggering deficit at over $18 million. From this study, Miller gained ideas on stabilizing the economy and improving the efficiency of state government, particularly its financial methods. He advocated raising the borrowing limit of the state to $3 million and issuing bonds up to $20 million. A $25 million bond issue for roads was defeated, and even Miller rescinded his support of this as too expensive. He also recommended a two-cent gasoline tax, which was later reduced to one cent per gallon and passed.

At this time, Governor Miller proposed the controversial state income tax which brought about a virtual rebellion in the senate. Many of the legislators felt a sales tax would be more effective. Miller considered the sales tax as too much a burden on the little man, and the income tax to be a levy largely against the higher income groups who could afford to pay.

The summer of 1931 was long and hot, especially in the legislative chambers of Alabama. Finally, the income tax measure emerged from the senate, only to be questioned again by the courts as possibly unconstitutional. (An income tax had been passed by the legislature in 1919 and declared unconstitutional by the state supreme court.)

None of this daunted Miller. He tried again with an extra session of the legislature in August, 1932, and again the income tax was defeated, along with a heavy bond issue. It should be noted as credit to the legislature that the defeat was largely because no rate limits were included as a ceiling on the tax.

The governor summoned the legislature again on January 31, 1933, and this time hammered the income tax amendment through. In July, it was finally submitted to the vote of the people and, along with the amendment repealing prohibition, was passed into law. This final income tax measure, with ceiling limits, was incorporated into the new budget system and became part of the state constitution. Miller evidently was wise enough to realize that if a state sales tax had been allowed, he would never have achieved passage of his income tax measure.

Also in the 1931 legislature, a state inheritance tax was adopted which reclaimed much of the estate taxes which had previously gone to the federal government.

It should be pointed out that the legislature, especially during the sessions of 1931 and 1932, was most uncooperative with Miller's stringent plans for economy, refusing consistently to limit the lawmakers' own expenses, even after salaries of state officials and employees had been drastically reduced. However, in the legislative session of 1933, the representatives finally voted to reduce their own expenses and, in addition to the income tax, they passed a $19 million warrant issue to fund the floating debt with the income tax revenues to be applied against this amount until paid. Little by little progress was being made, and it was Miller's uncompromising stand which achieved it.

The act of unquestioned merit was the Budget Control Act of 1932 which held state spending within the limits of state income. This control measure, together with a strict budget within all state departments and a Convict Department virtually self-supporting through farm and cotton mill production, succeeded in bringing

Alabama through one of her worst financial crises since Reconstruction.

In addition, much legislative and executive action was necessary to accommodate the Roosevelt New Deal. The TVA was established, the Agricultural Adjustment Administration regulating farm production was established, and a considerable bit of relief monies through various agencies had to be coordinated through state government.

Governor Miller served his state well in extraordinarily difficult times. Perhaps not a man given to brilliant concepts, the income tax and Budget Control Act stand as representatives of his most far-reaching and creative innovations. But he was strong, honest beyond question, unyielding; and few would deny that Benjamin Meek Miller's sobriquet "The Oak of Camden" was totally deserved. He died February 6, 1944, at Selma.

FRANK MURRAY DIXON
(1939–1943)
Jefferson County

A brilliant newcomer upon the Alabama political scene had given the veteran politico Bibb Graves a hard, close fight for the governorship in 1934. He was Frank M. Dixon of Birmingham. When the votes were totaled that summer day in June following the run-off, Graves had won by less than 22,000 votes. Graves mopped the cold sweat from his brow and reentered the governor's office. Frank Dixon began to plan his campaign for 1938. That race he won easily, and the old political order gave way to the new.

Dixon had the ardent support of Grover C. Hall, Sr., Pulitizer Prize winning editor of the Montgomery *Adver-*

tiser. Dixon threw away the old book with its stereotypes, its grinding axioms, its chauvinistic generalizations; and like the point of a sword, he sent his message into the hearts of Alabamians, especially the young. He talked about reality, he gave facts and figures; he bemoaned the desultory pace at which Alabama had kept behind in its economic and social planning and in the cumbersome administration of its government. He cited the modern up-to-date organization of the state of Virginia and showed in fascinating detail how waste, duplication, inefficiency, and inordinate costs might be eliminated in Alabama by following such a plan.

Dixon was patrician, he was handsome, and his oratory was magnificent. He was an aristocrat in every sense of the word, aristocratic in character and achievement, as well as in bloodlines which reached far back into this country's early history to the old dominion state of Virginia.

Frank Murray Dixon was born on July 25, 1892, in Oakland, California, the son of Frank and Launa Murray Dixon. For three generations back, his forebears on both sides had produced Baptist preachers and distinguished lecturers. He was the grandson of author Thomas Dixon, who wrote *The Klansmen,* the book from which "The Birth of a Nation" was adapted.

His early education was in the public schools of Dixondale, Virginia and Washington, D.C. He later attended Phillips Exeter Preparatory School, studied at Columbia University, and received his law degree from the University of Virginia in 1916.

He began law practice that same year in the Birmingham office of Frank S. White; from 1919 to 1939, he was a partner in the legal firm of Bowers and Dixon of Birmingham. In November of 1920, he married Juliet Perry of Greene County and Birmingham. From 1919 to 1923,

Dixon was assistant solicitor of Jefferson County. In 1929, he authored and published a legal tract entitled "The Local Laws Relating to Jefferson County."

In World War I, Dixon volunteered with the Canadian Air Corps. He was commissioned a second lieutenant and sent overseas in September, 1917. He was assigned to one of the French Escadrilles as aerial observer and machine gunner. He was wounded in July, 1918, and his leg was amputated as a result. He received the Croix de Guerre with Palm, was named a Chevalier of the French Legion of Honor, and attained the rank of major.

In evaluating the accomplishments of Dixon's administration, one must keep in mind that another war was going on, World War II, and it dominated every aspect of life for practically the whole period. This fact necessarily conditioned the limits of what could be done by any governor, anywhere.

Even so, Dixon was able to accomplish most of those governmental reforms and remodeling which he had promised in both his campaigns. The major change was a restructuring of the state governmental machinery which eliminated much of the duplication and excess costs by focusing the administrative power at one central point, in the office of the governor. Dixon also managed through his legislature to bring some similar improvement to the governments of Alabama counties and municipalities.

Perhaps next in importance was the introduction of a state civil service system and the elimination of the old spoils system, an ancient sore on the body politic. The "Little Hatch Act" went even further and made it illegal for nonelective employees of state, county, or municipal governments to campaign for political candidates.

The system of taxation in the state was modernized and the educational structure reorganized with the objective of bringing improved educational methods and tools into the classroom. Changes were made in the judicial system which streamlined court procedures—at least for that period.

Finally, Dixon licensed the sale of beer and wine and put into effect the package store method of dispensing hard liquors, with local option by county still in effect.

Among the giant contributions of Alabama to the war effort was the establishment of a host of military installations throughout the state. Brookley Field, a massive supply and repair depot in Mobile, was among them. The Selective Service Act was adopted by Alabama, as in other states, and its administration was of course a necessary function of the state government. Also, the vital Office of Price Administration, another federal wartime agency, had to be coordinated through state government.

The war itself was largely responsible for the rapid, widespread growth of industry in Alabama, but the impetus and guidance of this pell mell expansion fell largely to the state government. The average pay of a factory worker in Alabama had doubled by the end of the war. The Alabama State Docks at Mobile were vital and their administrative reorganization under Dixon increased efficiency. Between 1939 and 1944, the barge traffic through the intracoastal canal system increased by 400 percent. And in Mobile, the shipbuilding and repair industry mushroomed, with such giant firms as Ingalls and Alabama Dry Dock and Shipbuilding Corporation setting up shop in that port city.

Chauncey Sparks succeeded Dixon in the governorship in 1943, and responsibility for the war effort fell to him; but the main structure had been laid by Dixon.

Dixon returned to his law practice in Birmingham following his term as governor. He never entered politics again on a grand scale. It was almost as if the meteoric heat generated by his dynamic assault was too intense and the fires burned out after the one brilliant flash. The esteem in which he was held nationally was indicated by his election as chairman of the Southern Governors Conference, held while he was incumbent.

Dixon died October 11, 1965, in Birmingham.

CHAUNCEY M. SPARKS
(1943–1947)
Barbour County

A lifelong bachelor, an able lawyer, a man of conservative instincts, Chauncey Sparks took over leadership of the state during U.S. involvement in the largest and most far-flung war of history. Naturally, the vital priorities of the war dominated his administration, but Sparks was still able to effect several of the meaningful planks in his campaign platform, notably in the areas of education, agriculture, and economy.

Like many Alabama governors, Sparks had run and been defeated in a previous campaign before winning the election. He lost to Dixon in 1938 and won over James E. Folsom in 1942. In addition to the problems imposed by the great war, Sparks was confronted with that complex period of readjustment at the end of the war, late 1945 and all of 1946.

Chauncey M. Sparks was born in Barbour County, Alabama on October 8, 1884, the son of George Washington and Sarah Sparks, formerly of Georgia. He was educated in the public schools of Quitman County, Georgia and graduated from Mercer University in 1907, receiving his LL.B. from the same institution in 1910. He began the practice of the law of Eufala, Alabama that same year, and in 1911 he was appointed judge of the

Chauncey M. Sparks
1943–1947

James Elisha Folsom
1947–1951
1955–1959

Gordon Persons
1951–1955

John Malcolm Patterson
1959–1963

inferior court of Barbour County by Governor O'Neal. He served in that capacity until April of 1915.

In the years 1919–1923 and 1931–1939, Sparks represented Barbour County in the state legislature and was a longtime prominent Democrat, serving for several years as secretary of the Barbour County Democratic Executive Committee.

Sparks had thus been well schooled for his high political position, and upon his inauguration in 1943 he quietly set about his tasks as governor. In spite of the inflationary pressures of the war years, Sparks managed to double the educational appropriations in Alabama and was successful in signing the eight-month minimum school period term into law. The University Medical College was established in Birmingham, a modest institution which would grow into a giant medical center for medical education, treatment of patients, and research.

The appropriations for Alabama agriculture were more than doubled during the Sparks years, and several new farm experiment stations were established, to be administered by Auburn Agricultural College. At the same time, Auburn was able to set up a school of forestry, badly needed in a state where so much pulpwood is grown for the giant paper manufacturing industries.

The war brought massive industrial growth to Alabama, and consequent labor problems arose. It became necessary to reactivate the Alabama Department of Labor (originally created in the Graves administration, then dropped). Sparks also made a determined and partially successful fight against discriminatory freight rates, an old federal bugabear which had long penalized southern industry and agriculture.

A meaningful constitutional amendment was passed which provided for the legislature to convene at least once each two years rather than once in four years. But perhaps most remarkable of all the accomplishments of this able administrator was his successful effort to reduce the state debt even in those unsettled and inflationary times.

Sparks ran again for governor in 1950 and was defeated by Gordon Persons. He retired then to his law practice permanently. Sparks was a gentleman of the old school, quiet, dignified, a man of unquestioned integrity. He was an able administrator, but he lacked the imaginative flair and the creative concepts of the truly great statesman. He died November 6, 1968, in Eufala.

JAMES ELISHA FOLSOM
(1947-1951; 1955-1959)
Cullman County

In the 1946 gubernatorial run-off, James E. "Big Jim" Folsom squared off against Handy Ellis, a traditional courthouse politician. In his campaign speeches, Folsom promised to unify the state and "scrub out that Capitol building." "They can't stop us by stirrin' up hatred and suspicion and tryin' to divide race against race, class against class," he said. "We just finished fightin' a war against hatred and violence. So now we're startin' a good neighbor policy right here in Alabama."

Folsom pledged to "scrub out" the capitol by striking first at the autocratic power of the Black Belt by reapportioning the legislature. He would revise the constitution to bring it in line with the democratic principle it was supposed to represent. He would repeal the poll tax, he would provide free textbooks to every Alabama school child, and he would pave farm to market roads in every Alabama county.

Alabama voters responded, and Folsom went on to defeat orthodox Handy Ellis by a vote of almost two to one. The branchhead people were jubilant, along with the Negroes; and the "Big Mules," as Folsom called the entrenched powers of plantation, industry, and wealth, were depressed—and with good reason.

Folsom claimed that he had gotten the election back on a democratic basis. But one reason for his victory, which he too understood, was that the thousands of war veterans, returning with a mature and sober assessment of the home they had left, held nothing in politics to be sacrosanct any longer. They refused to be led by the nose. Folsom also had the convenient endorsement of organized labor.

Folsom was a giant-sized (six-foot eight-inch), twentieth-century model of the Populist tradition. Andrew Jackson was his hero, and George Wallace was, temporarily at least, his protégé and ultimately his political heir. Wallace was his campaign manager in the 1954 campaign and wrote a number of his speeches. Wallace asked Folsom to appoint him a member of the Board of Trustees of Tuskegee Institute, and Folsom obliged. This was considered a liberal move on Wallace's part at that time, but it was in the Folsom tradition.

Probably Folsom's strongest speech on behalf of justice for the Negro was delivered Christmas of 1949. He said in part, "As long as the Negroes are held down by deprivation and lack of opportunity, all other people will be held down alongside them. Let's start talking fellowship and brotherly love and doing unto others."

Somehow the people of Alabama must have heard him and many wanted to follow. In the 1954 campaign, Folsom won the Democratic primary with a vote of 305,-384, more than the vote for six other candidates combined, preempting any run-off. He defeated Thomas Abernathy in the general election by nearly three to one. Bibb Graves had been the only man before him to be elected to two four-year terms as governor.

In February, 1956, less than two years after the U.S. Supreme Court ruling on school desegregation, a black girl, Autherine Lucy, was admitted to the University of Alabama, the first Negro to be admitted in the 123-year history of the institution. Mobs began to form, mobs of rubber mill workers and red hill folk, as well as students. The mobs became violent, and Autherine Lucy had to leave the university in fear of her life. Folsom sent the Alabama Highway Patrol to the campus to maintain order, but they failed at that task. The law of the land was brushed aside, and an awful precedent was set. Folsom did not meet this challenge.

Soon after he took office in his first term, Folsom ran head on into a recalcitrant legislature. He was frustrated on two issues in particular—the repeal of the poll tax and the reapportionment of the legislature. However, the Alabama supreme court later upheld his reapportionment plan unanimously, affording him some consolation.

In other less politically sensitive areas, Folsom was more successful. He paved more than 3,000 miles of roads, including many miles of farm-to-market roads, in his first administration and more than doubled this in his second term. The minimum school term was set at nine months, and over 300 new school buildings were erected. Teachers' salaries were increased to an average of $1800 a year, and in the second administration increased again by an average of $600. The Wallace Act was passed, authorizing a number of new trade schools. The Ku Klux Klan was at last unmasked by state law (and without the masks they proved impotent). Old age assistance was nearly doubled. Under the Hill–Burton Act, Alabama began a vast program of hospital building, and new, more effective child labor laws were enacted. The second term was in general a continuation of those first term policies.

Folsom was not only a man of giant physical size, he was also a man of giant appetites; and his drinking (particularly in the second term) was on the gargantuan scale. This became more than amusement and subject for anecdotes to staid Alabamians, and when he became involved in a paternity suit in 1948, there appeared the first indication that some followers were turning away. Folsom was happily married to his pretty second wife, Jamelle Moore (his first wife, Sarah Carnley, had died in 1944), when this occurred and the suit came to nothing; but it, together with the legend of his drinking, had adverse political effect. His unrealistic presidential hopes of 1948 were completely squashed. He failed even in the race for delegate to the national Democratic convention.

Folsom's critics also pointed to the inordinately heavy expenditures in office for running the governor's mansion and the purchase of a state yacht. Folsom, in his boyish guilelessness, never tried to evade these accusations; he simply laughed and said he would plead guilty.

For a long time, Alabamians were able to accept this honesty, even admire it. But the political winds were blowing bleak and cold in the mid-fifties, and when Folsom made the mistake of inviting Adam Clayton Powell, a Negro Congressman from Harlem, to share a drink with him in the mansion on Perry Street, the white columns of the capitol trembled. The very sound of Congressman Powell's voice was acid to raw southern nerves. Perhaps Folsom was overconfident. Apparently it was at this point that Wallace realized Folsom was becoming a political liability to his own future plans.

But Big Jim never waivered in his ideals or his intentions. He fought the Dixiecrats and challenged the interposition resolution of his own legislature, appropriately dubbing its advocates "Nullicrats." Nevertheless, such were the changing sands upon which he stood that every

Alabama elector voted the third party ticket, carrying the state for Strom Thurmond, leaving the giant in bemused disbelief.

By the end of his second administration, the political tides had turned and his ideal world had gone from his reach. His mind, his perceptions were dulled with alcohol. It has been suggested that Folsom lacked the ruthlessness to be a great politician. Perhaps that is true, but even more he lacked a wide, objective view of the fickle nature of the passing throng.

James Elisha Folsom was born on a farm near Elba in Coffee County, October 9, 1908, the son of Joshua and Eulala Dunnevant Folsom. His father was a local politician, serving as deputy sheriff, tax collector, and member of the Coffee County Commission.

Folsom attended the schools of Coffee County and later the University of Alabama and Howard College for short terms. He served in the U.S. Merchant Marine from 1929 until 1932 and again for a year during World War II, after he was discharged from the army in 1943.

He worked with the Civil Works Administration in 1933 and later with the WPA in Washington; during this period he also studied political science and public speaking at George Washington University. In 1936 and 1938, Folsom ran for Congress and was defeated both times. Following these campaigns, he moved to Cullman County and began operation of an insurance business. In 1942, he was defeated in his first race for the governorship. But following his wartime service, he returned and made his triumphant race of 1946. On May 5, 1948, he was married to his second wife, Jamelle Moore.

Folsom ran again for governor in 1962, this time against the aspiring and tireless Wallace. There was a chance that he might have made a better showing, or even might have won, except for that fatal appearance on election eve to make a statewide telecast. To every one of the thousands of listeners, sitting awaiting amusement, revelation, something on the grand scale from the old-timer, it became painfully obvious that Big Jim was helplessly drunk. That was his political end.

He tried three times since then, the last time in 1974 against his old protégé, the seemingly invincible George Wallace.

There is a sadness here; but Big Jim had his day. He expressed something basically human, wild, and undisciplined, but full of compassion.

GORDON PERSONS
(1951–1955)
Montgomery County

A native Montgomerian and member of a distinguished Montgomery family, Gordon Persons came to the governorship via the Public Service Commission. His background in electrical engineering and his pioneer work in Alabama radio broadcasting made Persons an able head of this vital public service. He served on the commission for nine years and was its head when elected governor in 1950.

Gordon Persons was educated in the schools of Montgomery and later graduated from Auburn (then Alabama Polytechnic Institute) with a degree in electrical engineering. He went immediately into the field of radio broadcasting in which he wisely saw a future development of massive proportions. He operated one of Alabama's first public broadcast stations, WSFA of Montgomery.

Persons too made a first unsuccessful bid for the governor's chair. In 1946, he was pitted against the rising political strength of James Folsom and was defeated. In 1950, Persons made a second try against strong opposition, some dozen or more candidates, including former governor Chauncey Sparks, the Folsom-backed Phillip Hamm, and other veteran political campaigners. He led in the primaries, then easily won the run-off against Hamm.

It was appropriate and expected that in the Persons administration radio and television broadcasting would expand in the state. Two hundred sixty-eight educational channels were authorized by the Federal Communications Commission. A Commission for Educational Television was authorized by the Alabama legislature; funds were appropriated and Alabama became a pioneer in the field, with its first educational television broadcast made from atop Mt. Cheaha, the highest point in Alabama, in January of 1955.

Under pressure of the constant growth of population and the need for additional schools, the legislature approved and presented to the people a bond issue of $100 million for construction of school buildings. The sales tax was raised during Persons' administration from 2 to 3 percent to provide additional revenues for the schools; in 1951 each public school teacher received an increase of $300 a year. An additional bond issue for $25 million was also passed for new and improved highways throughout the state.

Persons seems to have been a man of high ideals and humanitarian instincts. Soon after his inauguration, he made a display on the capitol grounds of burning the straps used in corporal punishment of convicts. He gave his total backing to the state Highway Patrol and led a campaign against speeders and careless drivers. The famous U.S. Supreme Court decision of 1954—Brown vs Board of Education—outlawed segregation in public schools, but apparently little was done in Alabama either conforming to or opposing this new ruling under Persons.

Governor Persons' administration might be classified as moderately progressive and low key. However, there was little in it which indicated his mind grasped the imaginative and creative concepts vital to leadership at the highest levels of state government.

He was married to the former Alice McKeithen of Montgomery.

Following an extended illness, Governor Persons died in Montgomery on May 29, 1965.

JOHN MALCOLM PATTERSON
(1959–1963)
Russell County

John Malcolm Patterson, forty-sixth governor of Alabama, was another of the young World War II veterans elected to the governorship. His record in law school, his work as attorney general of the state from January, 1955 until January, 1959, and his natural penchant for executive leadership all seem to have well qualified Patterson for the office. He had an outstanding war record, and he was particularly well known because of the tragic 1954 assassination of his father, attorney general-elect, a man who had made a courageous fight against the then rampant organized crime in Phenix City.

Patterson had a brilliant political beginning; and his early political demise was due largely to the phenomenon of George Wallace and his rapid ascendancy to an impregnable position of political power in Alabama.

During his term, Patterson accomplished much that was positive for the progress of the state and its various institutions, particularly educational institutions. But perhaps he is remembered best as the implacable foe of integration; in fact, there had not been up to his time so shrill and vehement a political voice on the matter. The school integration ruling of the Supreme Court in 1954 hung in the air like the sword of Damocles when Patterson took office as attorney general in January, 1955, and his act of banishing the NAACP from the state set the pace for his subsequent uncompromising stand. For a time, it was an effective political maneuver (witness his unprecedented victory in the governor's race), but for the long run it was a mistake which hurt not only Patterson but all Alabama. This holding action only complicated and made more difficult the inevitable.

John M. Patterson was born September 27, 1921, at Goldville, Tallapoosa County, Alabama, son of Albert L. and Agnes Louise Benson Patterson. He attended schools at Rockford, Alexander City, and Phenix City, where he graduated from Central High School.

Following a long World War II military career, beginning in March, 1940, and including service in the Seventeenth Field Artillery Battalion and participation in the Tunisian, Sicilian, Italian, southern France, and German campaigns, he was discharged with the rank of major on January 6, 1946. He again served as an artillery officer in the Korean War, earning a reserve commission as lieutenant colonel in the Army Reserve Corps.

Patterson entered the University of Alabama in 1945, majored as an undergraduate in political science, and received his law degree from the university's School of Law in 1949. He entered the practice of law in Phenix City that same year.

On October 19, 1947, Patterson, a Methodist, was married to Mary Jo McGowin of Clanton.

He was selected to serve on the editorial board of the Alabama Law Review and became a member of the Farrah Order of Jurisprudence. In 1956, he was selected as one of the Outstanding Young Men of the Nation by the National Chamber of Commerce.

With the assassination of Patterson's father just prior to the general election in November, 1954, the state Democratic Executive Committee saw fit to name John Patterson the fill-in Democratic candidate, and he was elected. During his.four years as attorney general, Patterson made a favorable impression as an aggressive and courageous fighter against crime. Bolstered by wide voter sympathy for the cruel death of his father, he was a natural choice for the Democratic nomination for governor in 1958.

There were fourteen candidates in the race, the strongest being Patterson, Jimmy Faulkner, and George C. Wallace. However, Patterson led the field in a record total vote of 618,000, Wallace running second. In the run-off on June 3, Patterson defeated Wallace with the largest majority in Alabama political history to that time —64,902 votes. He easily defeated the Republican candidate in November and was inaugurated on January 20, 1959.

An interesting consideration in the election was Patterson's acceptance of Klan support and Wallace's refusal of it. In fact, Wallace wound up with the endorsement of the NAACP, the political kiss of death at that time.

Patterson proved to be a strong executive and had the support of his legislature in most instances. His accomplishments were legion. A $60 million highway bond issue was passed during his term and 1200 miles of new highways were constructed. River transportation facilities were improved, including new construction and ma-

Lurleen Burns Wallace
1967–May, 1968

Albert Preston Brewer
1968–1971

George Corley Wallace
1963–1967
1971–1975
1975–

chinery at the Mobile docks; and the inland docks at Decatur and Huntsville began operation.

In aid to education, Patterson broke the records. August, 1959, saw passage of the largest educational appropriation in the state's history—$148 million for one fiscal year alone. Thirty million dollars in new taxes was raised and earmarked for education; all public school teachers received an across the board 15 percent pay raise; and a bond issue of $100 million was authorized for construction of new school buildings.

Additional monies were appropriated for state hospitals for the mentally ill; stricter laws were passed regulating loan companies and curtailing loan shark practices. Legislation increases in old age pensions initiated free hospital care for the aged.

It was an impressive record for a young and aggressive governor. His future looked good to his supporters; but George Wallace was out on the hustings in his shirt sleeves, and John Patterson could not, under law, succeed himself. By the time Wallace had served his four years, he was able to have his wife succeed him in a race that saw the political end of the trail for the veteran Folsom and for the neophyte Patterson.

After his tenure as governor, John Patterson practiced law in Montgomery.

LURLEEN BURNS WALLACE
(1967–May, 1968)
Tuscaloosa County

The ultimate test of George Wallace's power at the Alabama voting booths came in 1966 when his wife Lurleen ran as his stand-in. She not only ran, but she won the Democratic primary, polling 54 percent of the vote against nine opponents, including two former governors, Folsom and Patterson. In the November general election, she brushed aside the Republican, James Martin, receiving 65 percent of the vote. She then became the first woman governor in Alabama history and the third in all the fifty states; circumstances considered, it was an unparallelled phenomenon in U.S. political history.

There was never any question but that Lurleen was running for George Wallace, and, when elected, that she would run the office of governor under his direction. They both were candid about the matter, and the voters understood this arrangement perfectly. Wallace had been unsuccessful, by a narrow margin, in persuading the legislature to amend the constitution of 1901 so that he might succeed himself. This maneuver was his answer, his political gamble to retain the reins of government and the power structure he had built. Mrs. Wallace presented throughout the campaign a demeanor of quiet charm; dressed simply, diminutive, pretty, dignified, she was very much a lady. Her speeches were short and usually preceded longer speeches "on the issues" by Wallace himself. The Alabama voters went for it like grits and gravy.

In office, she carried out the Wallace policies already established. On her own initiative, she instigated policies which improved conditions in the state's hospitals for the mentally ill. In 1967, her administration undertook the largest road building program in Alabama history to that time and began a gigantic park and recreation program.

She made one dramatic public appearance in the spring of 1967, a televised speech to the legislature proclaiming resistance on the part of Alabama to the federal guidelines for integration. Whatever the import and design of the speech, she delivered it with force and fault-less elocution.

She had, for a long time, even before the campaign, been suffering with a worsening condition of cancer. Her courage and steadfastness under pressure of the office, combined with her illness, left a lasting admiration among the people of Alabama. She died on May 7, 1968. A crusade to honor her memory was begun soon after her death; by 1970, over $5 million had been donated to the Lurleen Wallace Cancer Foundation for research.

Lurleen Burns Wallace was born on September 19, 1926, at Foster, Tuscaloosa County, Alabama, daughter of Henry Morgan and Janie Estelle Burroughs Burns. She attended the public schools of Tuscaloosa County and Tuscaloosa and graduated from Tuscaloosa County High School in 1942.

She then attended a business school and for a while worked in the offices of the Boy Scouts of America. While working as a sales clerk in a Tuscaloosa retail store, she met George Wallace, then awaiting induction into the military service. They were married May 22, 1943, in Tuscaloosa and honeymooned at his old home in Clio, Alabama. They were to have four children.

During Wallace's stateside service in the Army Air Corps, she stayed with him, whenever possible, living sometimes under trying conditions. After the first baby, Bobbie Joe, was born, she joined her husband in Alamogordo, New Mexico, and the best quarters they could afford was a renovated chicken house. When he was sent overseas in 1944, she returned to Alabama to sit out the war.

Following his return in late 1945, George Wallace began his political climb which took him to the governor's chair in January, 1963, and Lurleen became the state's First Lady, a position she graced with simplicity and dignity.

Lurleen Wallace was a courageous woman who gave everything to her family, to her husband, and to his career.

ALBERT PRESTON BREWER
(May, 1968–1971)
Morgan County

On May 7, 1968, following the death of Governor Lurleen Wallace, Lieutenant Governor Albert P. Brewer became governor of Alabama, at age thirty-nine the second youngest man ever to hold that office.

Brewer entered the office with an impressive background of governmental experience and proved himself an able, fair, and progressive executive. Brewer, a thin, modest man of patrician feature and quiet force, managed to bring a degree of stability and harmony into state government following the turmoil of the sixties. He reorganized the executive branch to effect more economy and efficiency; his leadership provided a far-reaching educational program, including $100 million in appropriations and a complete revamping of the state's educational system.

By the end of his term, he had earned widespread respect and had made a strong bid for an additional term in 1970, but he was defeated by the indomitable Wallace in the Democratic primary run-off of June.

Albert Preston Brewer was born October 26, 1928, on a small Tennessee farm near Bethel Springs; his parents, Daniel A. and Clara Yarber Brewer, moved the family in 1935 to Decatur, Alabama. Albert was the oldest of four children.

He attended the public schools in Decatur, became interested in civics and government, and made up his mind early to pursue a career in law. He enrolled at the University of Alabama in 1946 and graduated from the law school in 1952. At the university, he met Martha Farmer of Chattanooga, Tennessee. Married in 1950, they have two daughters. Brewer is a Baptist.

Admitted to the bar in the year of his graduation, Brewer set off with his young family to establish law practice in Decatur. In 1954, he was elected to the legislature and was reelected twice in succession without opposition. In the beginning of his third term in 1963, he was elected speaker of the house, where he established a reputation as a fair and firm presiding officer. During his third term, he was also elected by the Capitol Press Corps as the "Outstanding Member of the House."

In the 1966 Democratic primary, Brewer won the nomination for lieutenant governor without a run-off; he was unopposed in the November general election. At the time, Brewer was in the Wallace camp.

Then, following Governor Lurleen Wallace's death, he moved into the governorship. He selected his cabinet and immediately began to restructure the executive branch in the name of economy and efficiency. A little over a year later, he was able to announce that the state had ended the fiscal year with over $16 million in the general fund.

In 1969, he called a special session of the legislature to meet the pressing need for improvements in the public school system. The legislature passed, almost in their entirety, his recommendations. His efforts to attract new industry resulted in approximately 45,000 new jobs.

Brewer was elected to the Executive Committee of the National Governors' Conference in 1969; he was vice-chairman of the Southern Governors' Conference.

Perhaps the clearest insight into Governor Brewer's accomplishments can be gotten from his own statement regarding his administration: "In a tangible way I believe my accomplishments would rank (1) a strong educational program . . . ; (2) the creation of the Alabama Development Office to coordinate and consolidate five areas of state government into this one agency designed to promote the economic development of the state; and (3) a strong business-like approach to state government with the elimination of brokers and agents doing business with the state at substantial additional expense particularly in the areas of highway purchases, general state purchases and state services, and the creation of the state motor pool."

After leaving the governorship, Brewer returned to the practice of law in Montgomery.

GEORGE CORLEY WALLACE
(1963–1967; 1971–   )
Barbour County

George Corley Wallace proved himself a political phenomenon when he was elected to a third term as governor in the 1974 election with some 85 percent of the vote. Not only was a third term for an Alabama governor unprecedented, but Wallace's dominance in Alabama politics has been unequaled, even by such a master politician as Bibb Graves. In reality, the 1974 election for governor was the fourth which Wallace won, because in 1966 his late wife, Lurleen Wallace, was elected as his stand-in. Only Franklin D. Roosevelt's election to a fourth term as President surpasses this achievement, and even Roosevelt did not get his wife Eleanor elected.

George Corley Wallace was born August 25, 1919 at Clio, Alabama, a country town in Barbour County near the southeastern edge of the Black Belt. His father was George C. Wallace, Sr., a farmer and sometimes county politician, who at the time of his death was chairman of the Barbour County Board of Revenue. His mother, Mozelle Smith Wallace, a woman of proud and unbending character, worked for twenty-two years in the state Department of Health and helped, as did George from his early boyhood, in the support of the family. George's grandfather was George Oscar Wallace, a country doctor and at one time probate judge of Barbour County. A man of great sympathy and understanding, Oscar Wallace was perhaps the greatest single influence on the young George, who spent much of his time as a child at his grandfather's home.

In early life, spent in the midst of the great Depression, Wallace met the challenge of unrelenting hard work. At age sixteen, he procured a job as page in the state legislature at Montgomery. The characteristics which were to mark his mature years early exhibited themselves—tireless energy, an implacable ambition and need to get his work done well, and a gregariousness which was to become one of his strongest assets.

As a boy, Wallace played the games that other country boys play—swimming, fishing, and, of course, baseball. And as was customary in rural Alabama in those days, Negro boys played side by side with the whites.

Though small of stature, Wallace was agile, aggressive, and strong—a good athlete. He was named captain of his high school football team, and in 1936 and 1937 he won the Southern Golden Gloves bantamweight boxing championship. He continued athletics in college, where he was an outstanding boxer and was named captain of both the boxing squad and baseball team.

When Wallace arrived on the campus of the University of Alabama in the fall of 1937, all he possessed was the suit he wore, a few dollars in his pocket, and some meager belongings in a cardboard suitcase. Even then, he apparently knew what he wanted to do in life; already he was a politician with Populist leanings. He refused to join a fraternity, preferring to identify with the less privileged, the little man.

He found a room at a boardinghouse, waited tables, did kitchen work, and later drove a taxi to pay his way. He soon became well known and, running as an independent, defeated the fraternity candidate for president of the Freshman Class. He drank almost nothing alcoholic, but consumed quantities of soft drinks at social occasions; he smoked cigars and apparently became famous for his prodigious consumption of catsup on almost any food.

Although he was popular, he was something of a loner, and even then drove himself toward his distant goal. When he graduated in 1942, he could not pick up his diploma because he was unable at the moment to pay some back student fees; but in the law school, he had been named to the highly prestigious Law School Honor Court.

With his law degree finally in hand, he was admitted to the Alabama bar in 1942 at age twenty-three. But there was a war going on, so Wallace volunteered for service in the U.S. Army Air Corps for cadet training. However, he was not inducted until January 31, 1943. In the interval he met Lurleen Burns in Tuscaloosa, where Wallace was still working, driving a truck. He proposed before he left for his induction, and she accepted. In cadet training at Arkadelphia, Arkansas, he contracted spinal meningitis and was hospitalized. Following his recovery, he came to Tuscaloosa on a fifteen-day furlough, and he and Lurleen were married there in May by a justice of the peace. They spent their honeymoon in Wallace's old home at Clio, and even then Wallace could not stay away from the people, wandering about old haunts, shaking hands, renewing old acquaintances.

After he returned to duty, Wallace was eventually assigned as flight engineer trainee with a B-29 group in Alamogordo, New Mexico. Following the birth of their first baby, Lurleen joined her husband and they took up housekeeping in the famous chicken coop. But the renovated chicken coop must have later seemed a palatial haven as George Wallace sat before the engine instrument board on "The Sentimental Journey," a B-29 winging its way high over the Pacific for bombing attacks on Japan. A few days before he was scheduled to return to the states from his base on Tinian, the first atomic bomb was dropped on Hiroshima; while he was in flight homeward, the second bomb was dropped on Nagasaki, and the long war came to an end.

Wallace rejoined Lurleen in Mobile on August 13, one day before VJ Day, and was discharged with the rank of sergeant on December 8. It was time for his political career to begin, and he knew it. He drove to Montgomery where he persuaded Governor Chauncey Sparks, also of Barbour County, to appoint him as an assistant attorney general.

That was only a first step. Wallace immediately began to run for the legislature and was elected in November, at the same time Jim Folsom was first elected governor. Wallace was twenty-seven. Apparently, he and Folsom were close at the time; both held Populist views, and George Wallace was to manage Folsom's second successful campaign for governor in 1954.

As a legislator, Wallace was aggressive and dedicated. He insisted on signing his own bills alone. And under his

authorship were some of the most progressive acts of the
day—an act setting up Alabama trade schools; another
creating the new state junior college system; another
which brought city and county employees under social
security and provided free tuition for children and widows of war casualties. At Wallace's own request, Folsom
appointed him a member of the Board of Trustees of
Tuskegee Institute, an all-black college at that time. In
1947, Wallace opened a law office in Clayton and in 1949
was joined in the firm by his brother Jack. In 1950, he was
reelected to the legislature without opposition. While he
was in the legislature, the Capitol Press Corps twice
voted him "Outstanding Member of the Legislature."

Wallace was considered at this time a member of the
liberal camp; and after the conservative Gordon Persons
took office as governor in 1951, Wallace ran into frustrating indifference and hostility. He thereupon left the
legislature in 1953 and got himself elected as judge of
the third judicial circuit, which included Barbour
County.

In this position, Wallace was apparently the first
judge to institute the policy of probation for some con-
victed defendants, especially Negroes who could not
afford a lawyer. And it was at this same time that he
began to speak out against pending civil rights bills before Congress. He was already running for the governorship.

In the last few weeks of his judgeship, Wallace had his
first encounter with federal authority. The United States
Civil Rights Commission requested the voting records of
his circuit, and Wallace flatly refused, threatening to jail
any agent who came after them. It became the duty of
Wallace's old college friend, Frank Johnson, then a federal district judge, to order release of the records. Wallace again refused and thereupon faced a charge of

contempt of court. Perhaps he realized he had gone too far, and he turned the records over to a hastily summoned grand jury in his circuit. Nevertheless, the charge of contempt was filed and Wallace pleaded guilty. He was acquitted, but with some dubious words from Judge Johnson as to Wallace's motives.

In 1958, he formally entered the governor's race and received more than a quarter million votes, placing second in the primary to Patterson. Patterson ran strong on the racial issue and accepted the support of the Ku Klux Klan; Wallace refused it. Ironically, Wallace thereupon received the endorsement of the NAACP. In the run-off, John Patterson led him by over 64,000 votes. Wallace vowed he would never be "outsegged" again.

He went back to his law practice in Clayton but never stopped running. During the whole four years, he was out on the hustings. In the primary of 1962, he defeated his old mentor Folsom, among others, and in the run-off he defeated the rising young politico Ryan DeGraffenreid.

In the general elections of November, Wallace polled the largest vote ever given a gubernatorial candidate in Alabama up to that time. His 1963 inaugural address ended with probably his most quoted phrases: "Segregation now! Segregation tomorrow! Segregation forever!" In view of the 1954 Supreme Court ruling, this seems incredible, but evidently Wallace meant to defy the federal dictates regarding integration, in spite of the handwriting on the wall.

It is unclear why Wallace felt it necessary to make his utterances so shrill, so vehement, and so easily adaptable by his critics to the concepts of demagoguery and racial bias. Certainly, he knew the irreversible direction which history was taking and that he could not turn back the clock. But either purposefully or inadvertently, he managed to create a national image of himself as racist *par excellence,* not an easy image to change.

In short order, conflict began—racial demonstrations in Birmingham, along with the nationally publicized fire hoses and police dogs; desegregation of public schools in Macon County; and probably most dramatic of all, the "stand in the school house door."

Following Attorney General Robert Kennedy's visit to Montgomery and his interview with Wallace at the capitol, two black students, Vivian Malone and James Hood, both qualified by admission standards, made their appearance to enroll in the University of Alabama. But the stage had already been set, powers of both sides were waiting. The Alabama National Guard had been nationalized and were on hand in the wings. Governor Wallace took his stand at the front entrance of the University gymnasium auditorium where registration was being held. The walkway outside was an avenue of faces as Assistant Attorney General Nicolas Katzenbach made his way toward the door which Wallace blocked. As Katzenbach neared him, Wallace held up his hand, and the assistant attorney general stopped before him. There was a brief exchange of words, then both men departed, Katzenbach back down the walk, Wallace into the auditorium. Subsequently, without more ado, the two Negroes were enrolled in the university. Vivian Malone stayed on until she graduated.

During his first administration, Wallace made his first sortie into the North. In 1964, he entered the presidential primaries in Wisconsin, Maryland, and Indiana and showed a surprising strength, receiving as high as 43 percent of the vote.

Prevented by the law at that time from succeeding himself as governor, Wallace made a strong, almost desperate, effort in 1965 to have a special session of the

legislature authorize submission of the necessary constitutional change to the vote of the people. But he ran into
stubborn opposition with filibusters in the senate, and
when the issue finally came to a count, Wallace lost by
three votes.

This was too much, and Wallace prevailed on his wife
Lurleen to run as his stand-in. The only strong opposition to any Wallace candidate was Ryan DeGraffenreid,
making his second bid for the governorship. But De-
Graffenreid, while campaigning in mountainous northern Alabama, was killed in the crash of his small private
plane. After an appropriate period, Lurleen Wallace was
announced as a candidate for governor. She won with a
wide plurality.

In 1968, the year of his wife's death, Wallace again
entered the presidential campaign, was accepted on the
ballot in all fifty states, and won the primaries in Georgia,
Mississippi, Louisiana, Arkansas, and Alabama. He received, as candidate of the Independent party, some
10 million votes.

On February 26, 1970, he announced his candidacy
for a second term as governor and on June 2 beat incumbent Albert Brewer for the Democratic nomination. He
was inaugurated the following January, the same month
he married his second wife, Mrs. Cornelia Ellis Snively,
a stunningly beautiful and personable divorcee, niece of
former governor Jim Folsom.

In 1972, Wallace again entered the presidential primaries, this time within the Democratic party, and he led
off with a Florida victory in which he carried every county
in the state. In May, 1972, Wallace was campaigning in
Maryland. While moving through a crowd, shaking
hands, he walked into the sights of a .38 revolver held by
would-be assassin Arthur Bremer. Bremer opened fire at
short range, felling Wallace with three bullets in his

body, one partially severing his spinal cord and paralyzing both his legs. That ended his campaign, but he won
primaries in Maryland, Michigan, Tennessee, and North
Carolina, in addition to his Florida victory.

By August, Wallace had partially recovered from the
assassination attempt and he appeared at the Democratic
Convention in Miami. Soon he returned to his duties as
governor. In the Democratic primaries in May, 1974,
Wallace easily won the gubernatorial nomination for a
third term without a run-off. He subsequently was
elected by an overwhelming margin.

Wallace's record through 1974 includes some remarkable accomplishments as governor of Alabama. He
sponsored the largest highway expansion program in the
state's history. Eighty percent (635 miles) of the inter-
state system was complete by 1974 and some 4,000 state,
county, and city highway projects had been completed
since 1963. Federal revenue-sharing funds were used to
set up the Death Trap Elimination Program.

During his tenure, the Alabama Council on Arts was
established, and twenty-nine junior colleges and trade
schools were financed and set in operation. The University of South Alabama was established in Mobile in 1963,
with the addition of a four-year medical college in 1972.
He promoted the vast expansion of the medical facilities
at the University of Alabama Medical Center in Birmingham, and made a record educational appropriation during 1973–1974 of more than $500 million.

A record capital investment in Alabama industries in
1973 exceeded $1.5 billion, doubling the investment of
1972 and resulting in over 1,000 new or expanded plants
and approximately 43,000 new jobs.

Wallace also made vital improvements in the Alabama Law Enforcement Planning Agency, considered by

some experts to be a model. He doubled expenditures for improved health care, allocating revenue-sharing funds to mental health care.

By July 1, 1974, unemployment compensation and workmen's compensation showed a 130 percent increase for the decade. In 1972, the Alabama Office of Consumer Protection was established. In 1973, farm income exceeded $1.5 million, doubling that of 1972. Maximum old age pensions were raised to a figure of $115 per month.

Among these achievements, those of Wallace's second administration were realized without any exorbitant increase in state taxes.

During his administrations, Wallace has lived frugally in the Governor's Mansion, and he has found sufficient time to maintain close relations with his church. He is lay reader and a member of the Board of Stewards of the Methodist Church at Clayton.

A final evaluation of Governor Wallace at this time is, of course, impossible; even in his crippled condition he seems healthy, strong, and determined to continue his political career. And even if his political career were already ended, he is too controversial, too complex for any immediate and cursory judgment to be definitive. The historians and political writers will have this challenge before them for years to come.

Yet, a few general remarks are in order. The basic question to be answered for any in-depth understanding of the man seems to be this: Is he, as some critics avow, a racist demagogue, a bigot and political opportunist, motivated solely by ambition and bias, or have his actions been consistently motivated by his own belief that his views are right, both constitutionally and morally?

Certainly, no one can deny that political expediency played a large part in his racial stance during the 1962 campaign, and in some incidents which followed; but does that necessarily preclude an accompanying belief on his part in the constitutional principle he doggedly defended and has consistently defended ever since?

Does anything in his personal life, or even in his political life, indicate a hatred of blacks? Any fair evaluation would surely require a close examination of his record, not just his speeches.

His "stand in the school house door" was hopeless, and surely he knew this. He has repeatedly stated it was but a symbolic act on the part of a southern governor to raise a final specific issue for court consideration. Of course, the issue had already been decided, and his defiance seemed inordinately silly; but shortly after this, he made his first venture into the national presidential primaries, the results of which have been noted.

With the social revolution of the sixties behind him, Wallace seems to have moderated his views as to what he can and cannot do. If, as it seems, he has acceded gracefully to change, accepted what seemed only a few years ago inconceivable, he has done only what several million other southerners have done. The great incidents of violence during the revolution were not in the South, they were in the North. And the peaceable character of that change is a tribute to the character of the southerners, black and white.

What has Wallace accomplished by entering politics on the national level? He has brought before the American public a basic Populist view, a southern viewpoint regarding vital issues which apparently is shared by millions of Americans outside the South; and he has, through his political persuasiveness, forced both Democratic and Republican parties to hear him and to bend their platforms, to a degree, to accommodate those views.

Generally, his statements seem to indicate a strong belief in the freedom and dignity of the individual and in his right to handle his affairs through his local and state governments without bureaucratic dictation from Washington.

Wallace can speak with force, especially on broad principles; but his language is impaired by a basic halting inarticulateness—not just the roughhewn edges of speech which, in a different way, characterized Andrew Jackson's eloquence, but an awkward syntax which hinders the effectiveness of his speech.

Yet, perhaps language, though the best index to the quality of a man's mind, is not the final or even the best criteria for judging a man. What about character, those qualities which give it strength, such as courage, integrity, determination, compassion, and a common bond of spirit with the multitude? Are not these traits of character evident in George Wallace?

Without attempting to answer the questions surrounding George Wallace, one thought seems appropriate: Those who are most vocal in their criticism of the man, those who decry the fact that in the 1970s he has represented the South to the nation, those supremely educated, polished men and women carrying the vestiges of an old tradition or a new liberalism in their hearts—they seldom seek to represent southerners at all.

Where is that *noblesse oblige,* that aristocracy vested in character and public responsibility? The shadows of a few have passed in the pages of this book.

Where are their sons and daughters?

As T. S. Eliot, the great twentieth-century poet, warned in the last lines of "The Hollow Men":

> *This is the way the world ends*
> *This is the way the world ends*
> *This is the way the world ends*
> *Not with a bang but a whimper.*

Roster of Governors

THE INDIANS
(Time Unrecorded)

THE FRENCH
(1701–1763)

Pierre le Moyne, Sieur d'Iberville
Jean Baptiste le Moyne, Sieur de Bienville   1701–1713
Antoine de la Mothe, Sieur de Cadillac   1713–1716
L'Epinay   1717–1718
Jean Baptiste le Moyne, Sieur de Bienville   1718–1724
Pierre Dugue, Sieur de Boisbriant   (acting) 1724–1726
Etienne Perier   1726–1733
Jean Baptiste le Moyne, Sieur de Bienville   1733–1743
Pierre François de Rigaud, Marquis de
    Vaudreuil   1743–1753
Louis Billouart, Chevalier de Kerlerec   1753–1763

THE BRITISH
(1763–1780)

George Johnstone   1764–1767
Montforte Browne   (acting)   1767–1769
George Elliot   (suicide)   1769 (1 month)

Elias Durnford   (acting)   1769–1770
Peter Chester   1770–1780

THE SPANISH
(1780–1813)

Bernardo de Galvez   1780–1785
Don Estevan Rodriquez Miro   1785–1791
Francisco Luis Hector, Baron de Carondelet 1791–1797
Manuel Gayoso de Lemos   (died in office) 1797–1798
Sebastian de la Puerto y O'Ferril, Marquis de
    Casa Calvo (acting)   1799–1801
Don Juan Manuel de Salcedo   1801–1803
Vincent Folch   1803–1811
Francisco Maximiliano de St. Maxent   1811–1812
Mauricio Zúñiga   1812–1813

MISSISSIPPI TERRITORY
(1799–1817)

Winthrop Sargent   1799–1801
William Charles Cole Claiborne   1801–1805
Robert Williams   1805–1809
David Holmes   1809–1817

ALABAMA TERRITORY
(1817–1819)

William Wyatt Bibb   March, 1817–November, 1819

STATE OF ALABAMA
(1819–   )

William Wyatt Bibb   (died in office) November, 1819–
                                                July, 1820

Thomas Bibb	1820–1821
Israel Pickens	1821–1825
John Murphy	1825–1829
Gabriel Moore	1829–March, 1831
Samuel B. Moore	March, 1831–November, 1831
John Gayle	1831–1835
Clement Comer Clay	1835–July, 1837
Hugh McVay	July, 1837–November, 1837
Arthur Pendleton Bagby	1837–1841
Benjamin Fitzpatrick	1841–1845
Joshua Lanier Martin	1845–1847
Reuben Chapman	1847–1849
Henry Watkins Collier	1849–1853
John Anthony Winston	1853–1857
Andrew Barry Moore	1857–1861
John Gill Shorter	1861–1863
Thomas Hill Watts	1863–April, 1865
Lewis E. Parsons (interregnum)	June, 1865–December, 1865
Robert M. Patton	December, 1865–July, 1867
Wagner Swayne (military governor)	July, 1867–July, 1868
William H. Smith	July, 1868–November, 1870
Robert Burns Lindsay	1870–1872
David P. Lewis	1872–1874
George S. Houston	1874–1878
Rufus W. Cobb	1878–1882
Edward Asbury O'Neal	1882–1886
Thomas Seay	1886–1890
Thomas Goode Jones	1890–1894
William Calvin Oates	1894–1896
Joseph Forney Johnston	1896–1900
William James Samford (died in office)	1900–June, 1901
William D. Jelks	June, 1901–1907

Russell McWhortor Cunningham (acting)	1904–1905
Braxton Bragg Comer	1907–1911
Emmett O'Neal	1911–1915
Charles Henderson	1915–1919
Thomas E. Kilby	1919–1923
William W. Brandon	1923–1927
Bibb Graves	1927–1931
Benjamin Meek Miller	1931–1935
Bibb Graves	1935–1939
Frank Murray Dixon	1939–1943
Chauncey M. Sparks	1943–1947
James Elisha Folsom	1947–1951
Gordon Persons	1951–1955
James Elisha Folsom	1955–1959
John Malcolm Patterson	1959–1963
George Corley Wallace	1963–1967
Lurleen Burns Wallace (died in office)	1967–May, 1968
Albert Preston Brewer	1968–1971
George Corley Wallace	1971–

Bibliography

Adams, James Turslow. *The Epic of America.* New York: Triangle Books, 1941.

Alabama Official and Statistical Register. Montgomery: State Department of Archives and History, 1931, 1939, 1942, 1947, 1955, 1959, 1963, 1967.

Baldwin, Joseph G. *The Flush Times of Alabama and Mississippi.* New York: Peter Smith, 1853.

Birmingham *News*: Oct. 12, 1965.

Brewer, Albert P., Written interview, June 5, 1974.

Brewer, W. *Alabama: Her History, Resources, War Record, and Public Men, From 1540–1872.* Tuscaloosa: Willo Publishing Co., 1964.

Concise Dictionary of American History. New York: Scribners, 1962.

Cordell, Carlton. TV interview with George Wallace at Southern Governors Conference, Grand Hotel, Point Clear, Ala. "News Conference," WALA TV, June 30, 1974.

Delaney, Caldwell. *The Story of Mobile.* Mobile: Gill Press, 1962.

Deep South Genealogical Quarterly, Vol. 5, No. 2. Mobile: Mobile Genealogical Society, Inc., Feb., 1968.

Dictionary of American Biography. American Council of Learned Societies, 1936.

Durante, Will, and Ariel Durante. *The Story of Civilization.* Vols. VIII and IX *(The Age of Louis XIV* and *The Age of Voltaire).* New York: Simon and Schuster, 1963.

Douglas, Marjory Stoneman. *Florida: The Long Frontier.* New York: Harper and Row, 1967.

Eufaula *Tribune*: Nov. 7, 1968.

Frady, Marshall. *Wallace*. New York: World Publishing Co., 1968.

Fuller, Herbert B. *The Purchase of Florida*. (Reprint of 1906 edition) Gainesville: The University of Florida Press, 1964.

Hamilton, Peter J. *Colonial Mobile*. (Revised and enlarged edition, Mrs. R. D. H. Cannon) 1st National Bank of Mobile, 1952.

Hanna, Kathryn Abbey. *Florida, Land of Change*. Chapel Hill: University of North Carolina Press, 1941, 1948.

Higgenbotham, Prieur Jay. *Mobile! City by the Bay*. Ed. Cathy Patrick. Mobile: The Azalea City Printers, 1968.

McWilliams, Richebourg B. *Fleur de Lys and Calumet*. Baton Rouge: Louisiana State University Press, 1953.

Mason, David. *Caladonian Indians in Southeast Alabama, 1790–1815*. Private Manuscript.

Miller, William. *A History of the United States*. New York: Dell Publishing Co., 1958.

Moore, Albert Burton. *History of Alabama*. (Revised edition) University, Ala.: Alabama Book Store, 1934.

Montgomery *Advertiser*: Nov. 7, 1968.

Mowat, Charles L. *East Florida as a British Province, 1763–1781*. Gainesville: University of Florida Press, 1964.

Osborne, John. *The Old South*. Time, Inc., 1968.

Owen, Thomas M. *History of Alabama and Dictionary of Alabama Biography*. (4 vols.) Chicago: Clark Publishing Co., 1921.

Owsley, Stewart Chappell. *Know Alabama*. (3rd edition) Montgomery: Viewpoint Publications, 1970.

Patrick, R. W. *Florida Under Five Flags*. Gainesville: University of Florida Press, 1960.

Pickett, Albert J. *History of Alabama*. (2 vols.) Birmingham: Webb Book Co., 1900.

Pope, James M., Manager of Grand Hotel, Point Clear, Ala., site of Southern Governors Conference, 1973. Personal interview.

Reeves, Miriam G. *The Governors of Louisiana*. (3rd edition) Gretna, La.: Pelican Publishing Company, 1972.

Saunders, Col. James Edmonds. *Early Settlers of Alabama*. Baltimore: Genealogical Publishing Company, 1969.

Summersell, Charles Grayson. *Alabama History for Schools*. (4th edition) Montgomery: Viewpoint Publications, Inc., 1970

Tebeau, Charlton W. *A History of Florida*. Coral Gables, Fla.: University of Miami Press, 1971.

Wallace, George C. *Hear Me Out*. Anderson, S.C.: Droke House Publishers, 1968.

Index